D0087918

Cultural Awareness in Therapy with Trans and Gender Non-Conforming Adults and Older People

of related interest

Counselling Skills for Working with Gender Diversity and Identity
Michael Beattie and Penny Lenihan with Robin Dundas
ISBN 978 1 78592 741 6
eISBN 978 1 78450 481 6
Essential Skills for Counselling series

Theorizing Transgender Identity for Clinical Practice
A New Model for Understanding Gender
S.J. Langer
ISBN 978 1 78592 765 2
eISBN 978 1 78450 642 1

Counseling Transgender and Non-Binary Youth
The Essential Guide
Irwin Krieger
ISBN 978 1 78592 743 0
eISBN 978 1 78450 482 3

Lesbian, Gay, Bisexual and Transgender Ageing
Biographical Approaches for Inclusive Care and Support
Edited by Richard Ward, Ian Rivers and Mike Sutherland
ISBN 978 1 84905 257 3
eISBN 978 0 85700 537 3

Transgender Health
A Practitioner's Guide to Binary and Non-Binary Trans Patient Care
Ben Vincent, PhD
ISBN 978 1 78592 201 5
eISBN 978 1 78450 475 5

White Privilege Unmasked
How to Be Part of the Solution
Judy Ryde
ISBN 978 1 78592 408 8
eISBN 978 1 78450 767 1

CULTURAL AWARENESS in THERAPY with TRANS and GENDER NON-CONFORMING ADULTS and OLDER PEOPLE

A PRACTICAL GUIDE

Tavi Hawn, LCSW

Jessica Kingsley Publishers
London and Philadelphia

Disclaimer: The information contained in this book is not intended to replace the services of trained medical professionals or to be a substitute for medical advice. You are advised to consult a doctor on any matters relating to your health, and in particular on any matters that may require diagnosis or medical attention.

First published in 2020
by Jessica Kingsley Publishers
73 Collier Street
London N1 9BE, UK
and
400 Market Street, Suite 400
Philadelphia, PA 19106, USA

www.jkp.com

Copyright © Tavi Hawn, LCSW 2020

All rights reserved. No part of this publication may be reproduced in any material form (including photocopying, storing in any medium by electronic means or transmitting) without the written permission of the copyright owner except in accordance with the provisions of the law or under terms of a licence issued in the UK by the Copyright Licensing Agency Ltd. www.cla.co.uk or in overseas territories by the relevant reproduction rights organization, for details see www.ifrro.org. Applications for the copyright owner's written permission to reproduce any part of this publication should be addressed to the publisher.

Warning: The doing of an unauthorized act in relation to a copyright work may result in both a civil claim for damages and criminal prosecution.

Library of Congress Cataloging in Publication Data
A CIP catalog record for this book is available from the Library of Congress

British Library Cataloguing in Publication Data
A CIP catalogue record for this book is available from the British Library

ISBN 978 1 78592 838 3
eISBN 978 1 78592 664 8

Printed and bound in the United States

Dedication

For Chris, my heart—Thank you for being Home and believing in me. Team Hawn ftw. For Dolores Almuhja—Thank you for being the only human to ever show me unconditional love.

For Tydi Dansbury, Roxana Hernandez, Jamie Lee Wounded Arrow, and Blake Brockington and all those who are no longer with us on earth, but still light the way. For the elders, youth, and trans women of color who have fought for a better world and achieved so many wins.

To my trans, Two Spirit, gender non-conforming kindred. You (we) bring so much beauty, spiritual guidance, and fierce f***ing fortitude to this world. Thank you for your gifts and let's keep taking care of each other.

To All My Relations.

Contents

A Note on Terminology

Throughout this book, I will use the term "trans" as a general umbrella term sometimes. I will also use "gender non-conforming" (GNC) to ensure inclusion of those who don't identify with the word "trans." I may use the acronym TGNC2S in place of transgender, gender non-conforming, and Two Spirit. Two Spirit is a term developed by Native and Indigenous peoples in the 1990s to represent an Indigenous understanding of gender that embodies a masculine and feminine spirit (see the Glossary of Terms to learn more). I may use the acronym POC in place of "people of color." I may use an "x" to signify inclusion of all genders, such as when I write "folks" as "folx." At times, I will include stories to illustrate points.

I will be using myself or TGNC2S people I know with identities disguised for privacy.

Glossary of Terms

In the book I may alternate between several of these acronyms so that you can be used to recognizing them, as which acronyms are used can vary throughout publications.

Acronyms

2S (Two Spirit)

BIPOC (Black, Indigenous, People of Color)

GNC (Gender Non-Conforming)

TGNC (Trans, Gender Non-Conforming)

TGNC2S (Trans, Gender Non-Conforming, Two Spirit)

POC (People of Color)

QTPOC (Queer/Trans People of Color)

QTBIPOC (Queer/Trans Black, Indigenous People of Color)

HRT (hormone replacement therapy) A hormonal intervention to assist someone in aligning their body and gender identity.

Terms

Affirming Absolute support for a person's gender identity or expression (in a society, this would mean that systems included, represented, and honored all genders).

All gender (as in "all gender restrooms") Signifying knowledge of, and inclusion of, multiple genders.

Anti-trans bias or discrimination Negative attitudes and beliefs about transgender people. These beliefs lead to a range of actions that deny transgender people full access to spaces, situations, and opportunities, as well as inflicting harm.

Biological sex The sex assigned to someone at birth, or prior to birth, via visual inspection of the genitals using ultrasound or eyes. Some still say there are two biological sexes, despite the fact that there can be a range of combinations of chromosomes, hormones, and genitals, as well as evidence of a spectrum of sex found in nature.

Boi/Gui Someone with masculine gender expression or identity, usually used in communities of color.

Cisgender ("Cis" is the abbreviation) An adjective describing a person whose gender identity aligns with the sex they were assigned at birth.

Cis-normative Worldview in which cisgender people are viewed as "normal" or "preferred."

Demi-boy Someone who identifies as mostly male, but not fully.

Folx The x replaces the s in "folks" to represent acknowledgement of multiple genders. (I have an acquaintance who thinks this is silly and pretentious. I alternate between using folks and folx, and still think there's value in signaling inclusion since most people using folks are still assuming there are only two genders.)

Gender affirming hormone therapy Sometimes used instead of HRT to emphasize the affirming and therapeutic aspect of hormones, versus viewing it as "replacement."

Gender binary The idea that gender is either male or female based on sex assigned at birth.

Gender expression A person's outward gender presentation, through means such as name, pronouns, hairstyle, clothing, accessories, body language, etc. Gender expression does not always align with gender identity and also does not have to be static or the same each day.

Gender neutral (as in gender neutral housing) Something that is not segregated by gender or assigned sex.

Gender non-conforming A person whose gender expression is different than cultural norms and expectations for that gender (for example, a feminine man or masculine woman). Not all trans people are gender non-conforming and not all gender non-conforming people identify as transgender.

Genderqueer One whose gender is neither just male or just female (outside of binary gender).

Hetero-normative Worldview in which heterosexuality is "normal" or "preferred."

Intersex or differences of sex development A category that describes a person with a genetic, hormonal, reproductive, or genital combination that is different than the "male" or "female" sex that doctors assign at birth. There are many of these conditions and they are not extremely rare (remember the whole "spectrum of biological sex found in nature"?). A person may or may not be aware of having an intersex condition. Some people may identify as "intersex" and others may identify as male, female, or any other gender.

Medical transition A range of medical options utilizing hormone therapy and/or surgical interventions to help a person's body more align with their gender identity.

Microaggressions Acts of dismissal or hostility (towards TGNC2S or POC) which can be intentional or unintentional. The term was coined by Chester Pierce to describe these acts towards Black people by non-Black people.

Pubertal suppression A reversible medical process that delays the onset of puberty for young adolescents to prevent increased dysphoria that can often come with puberty and to allow for decision-making about hormone therapy.

Social transition A trans person's process of making changes to have more of their life align with their gender identity. This can include things like asking others to use a new name or pronouns, changing style of dress or hair, etc. This could take place in various areas of a person's life (friends, family, school, work, faith community, cultural community, etc.)

Trans (abbreviation for transgender)

Transfeminine A trans person with feminine identity or expression who may or may not identify as female.

Transgender Adjective describing a person whose gender identity does not align with assigned sex at birth.

Transmasculine A trans person with masculine identity or expression who may or may not identify as female.

Two Spirit A pan-Indian term used by Native and Indigenous peoples to describe a gender that contains both masculine and feminine spirit and traits. It is used by some to describe their sexual orientation as well. Some believe that Two Spirit involves a spiritual and cultural role in addition to an identity. Others may not use the term Two Spirit and may instead use a tribal specific term.

Winkte A Lakota word referencing a two-souled person, or one who is like a woman.

Introduction

"I hold the status of several minorities: I cannot allow myself to be fragmented into Negro at one time, woman at another, and worker at another." (Pauli Murray, reprinted with permission of the Charlotte Sheedy Literary Agency)

"I knew I was different, then as much as now. But I didn't know until later that it was because I'm part heir to the Indian culture, and that small part has leavened the whole lump... And truly, I feel split between...cultures, not fully belonging [anywhere]." (Diane Clancy, reproduced from *I Tell You Now: Autobiographical Essays by Native American Writers*, edited by Brian Swann and Arnold Kropat. Copyright 1987 by the University of Nebraska Press)

"I have heard Indians joke about those who act as if they had no relatives, [and] I wince, because I have no relatives. They live, but they threw me away—so, I do not have them. I am without relations. I have always swung back and forth between alienation and relatedness." (Wendy Rose, reproduced from *I Tell You Now: Autobiographical Essays by Native American Writers*, edited by Brian Swann and Arnold Kropat. Copyright 1987 by the University of Nebraska Press)

This book provides guidance on practicing intersectional (the term created by Kimberle Crenshaw) care with transgender, gender non-conforming, and Two Spirit (TGNC2S) peoples. There is a great need for therapies, treatments, and settings that enable and encourage individuals to bring their whole selves for healing. Intersectional care honors all aspects of identity and endeavors to understand how those identities inform experiences throughout life. This book acknowledges that we cannot address only one part of a person and be relevant. We cannot focus on gender identity to the exclusion of other social identities. We must strive to understand all of the ways in which a particular person encounters the world, especially in light of multiple forms of societal oppression. We have to be able to examine the ways that overlapping systems of discrimination and inequity converge in the daily lives of individual people that we work with.

The Combahee River Collective, a Black, feminist, lesbian organization, discussed in their 1977 statement the importance of focusing on all of their identities in the struggle for liberation from oppression. Their understanding was that, by freeing those with the most marginalized identities, then everyone else would experience greater freedom as well (Combahee n.d.). My hope is that people reading this book will decide to share this framework and approach.

An intersectional stance in mental healthcare and social service work is crucial in order for a provider to assist people holding oppressed identities in avoiding internalizing blame and negative messages related to their systemic oppression (Adames *et al.* 2018).

It can be uncomfortable to consider privilege and oppression. It can be uncomfortable to consider new ideas. In reading this book, you may feel discomfort and that means you are open and learning. If you feel comfortable, or nothing at all, when reading this book, you are possibly operating with complacency or over-confidence. If you feel shame, you may shut down and that prevents us from learning. So, discomfort can be a good thing, and, in fact, we have to be able to bring these topics into the therapy room or our healing practice. Discomfort is a feeling we should be able to tolerate and accept.

Lastly, as stated by Robbins and McGowan (2016), an inter-sectional approach to trauma informed care brings to the forefront activism, advocacy, and social justice movements. These will be present in the lives of both clients or patients and providers, or at least actively discussed in sessions and meetings.

This moment in time

The majority of this book was written on Piscataway land and the traditional lands of the Susquehannock on Turtle Island, that is today home to many Lumbee, Piscataway, Cherokee, and other Native peoples. It was written mostly in the city where in 2015 the Freddie Gray uprising occurred, after Gray died of injuries while being transported by Baltimore Police Department, and officers were acquitted even though the medical examiner ruled the death a homicide. This is the same city where in 2018 Tydi Dansbury became at least the seventeenth Black trans person murdered in the year. The national Black Lives Matter movement continues to bring attention and social conscience to the history of racist violence towards Black folks.

At the time of writing this introduction, we have just come out of the longest government shutdown in US history over disagreement about proposed funding for a "Border Wall." This shutdown disproportionately affected Native and Indigenous peoples, whose funding for medical, mental health services, and basic assistance is tied to federal funding based on treaty agreements. Transgender asylum seekers from Central and South America are having difficulty finding US sponsors so that they can be released from detention centers, and Trump has ended Deferred Action for Childhood Arrivals (DACA) and protections for around 700 million DACA recipients, many of whom are LGBTQ+. The courts have upheld the "Transgender Military Ban." There are rallies and protests to raise awareness of missing and murdered Indigenous women (MMIW), highlighting that Indigenous women and Two Spirit people are significantly over-represented amongst the number of missing persons and homicides throughout Canada and the United States (reports from Canada in 2011 cite that Indigenous women and Two Spirits are seven times more likely to die of homicide than other racial groups; Mahony, Jacob, & Hobson 2017). Students from Parkland High School in Florida organized nationwide school walkouts, press conferences, and rallies for gun control after yet another mass school shooting, while groups such as Black Youth Project (BYP) 100 formed in response to the 2013 acquittal of the shooter of Trayvon Martin, age 12 at the time of his death, and have been tirelessly highlighting the murders of youth of color, without the same national media recognition. Water protectors are at Wet'suwet'en, Bayou Bridge, and Line 3 as pipelines continue to be woven through the northern hemisphere. Puerto Rico is still largely without power. There is currently a genocide occurring in Syria, by the Syrian military with Russia's support, and in Chechnya there has been an LGBTQ+ purge with suspected LGBTQ+ people being jailed, tortured, and killed. Trump has signed executive orders banning refugees from specific countries, which hurts LGBTQ+ individuals seeking to escape life-threatening oppression due to their identities.

Currently, the United States is living under the most actively anti-transgender presidential administration in its history. These are just a few of the hateful attacks on trans people carried out by this administration to date:

- the Department of Justice and Education withdrew the 2016 Title IX guidance informing schools on protection of transgender students

- the Department of Justice stopped enforcement of the Affordable Care Act's non-discrimination protection for transgender people

- the Department of Justice withdrew its lawsuit challenging North Carolina's anti-trans House Bill 2

- the Department of Housing and Urban Development announced it was withdrawing agency policies protecting LGBTQ+ people experiencing homelessness

- the Census Bureau refused to collect demographic information on LGBTQ+ people in the 2020 census

- Trump announced on Twitter that the military would no longer accept transgender people (largely impacting Black, Indigenous, people of color [BIPOC] trans folx)

- the Justice Department released a "license to discriminate" or "religious refusal" right to even illegal discrimination in government and private business

- the Department of Health and Human Services proposed religious refusal rights for healthcare workers who do not want to serve transgender people

- the Bureau of Prisons rolls back existing protections for transgender inmates, stating they must now be housed according to sex assigned at birth

- Trump and Congress overturned protections for Planned Parenthood, which widely serves the transgender community in various forms of healthcare.

At the time of writing this introduction, it's the one year anniversary of the *Black Panther* movie, and I've happily learned that Tomi Adeyemi's "Children of Blood and Bone" will be a series. Janelle Monae's *Dirty Computer* videos came out (and Janelle came out, teaching more of the population what "pansexual" means); Amanda Stenberg (Rue of *Hunger Games*) is out as non-binary and pansexual; Two Spirits Sean Snyder and Adrian Stevens took second place in the Sweethearts Special at the Seminole Tribal Fair pow wow; a record number of transgender political candidates entered 2017 races and five won, including Andrea Jenkins, a trans woman of color in Minneapolis. Trans communities are working hard at the local level to create resources and protect rights. Several states have passed legislation allowing birth certificates without assigned gender and ID documents that give an option for "non-binary," "unspecified," or "X" gender markers.

So, as always, in the midst of turmoil and trials, there is surviving, there is even thriving. These things occur in the same space in time, being experienced by the same people.

Why this book

The majority of graduate programs today that are training social workers, counselors, and psychologists offer little to no education on working from a culturally responsive framework. There is not an anti-racist, LGBTQ+ affirming curriculum in most of our universities and graduate programs. Not only is this harmful to the students in these programs who hold marginalized identities, but it doesn't prepare professionals to provide appropriate care. Over the years of giving talks and workshops to other professionals, I've noticed that people often want "concrete skills"; formulas or a manualized treatment to take back to their practices. While I understand this desire, I would argue that it stems from Eurocentric methods of teaching and learning, while other cultural groups or ethnicities may value methods such as story-telling or overall concepts and values that guide decision-making and that these are as valid as "skills."

This book attempts to bridge some of the gaps that I experienced in my own graduate training, as well as the ones I've observed and experienced when teaching as an adjunct professor in a large social work institution. In my own graduate program we had only one class where we discussed sexual orientation and racism. There was no mention of gender identity. When we discussed racism, there was no mention of Native and Indigenous peoples and very little mention of multiple ethnicities. I only had three professors of color during my training. When I taught a first year required macro social work class introducing community organizing and advocacy work, only 5 of 35 students in the class were students of color. There were no "out" LGBTQ+ students in the class. The students told me that no other professors besides me that year were giving them the opportunity to share their pronouns and preferred names or discussing how those things can change even in the course of a semester. These experiences echo many that I've heard from other providers about their own training. If this book can supplement the curriculum for students or offer continuing education for providers, I would be so humbled and happy.

My dream is that this book may also prevent some of the following things clients of mine have experienced with other providers.

- Psychiatrist to me about a shared client: "I've tried to convince [him] not to transition because [he] just isn't going to make a pretty woman."

- Different psychiatrist "evaluation" letter required by a large gender clinic for my client to proceed with a medical intervention (and copy given to my client to read) that said "patient is awkward and womanly…does not have typical male mannerisms and presentation but identifies as male."

- Client who had tried to talk about gender affirming hormone therapy options with a previous therapist and been told "maybe you should focus on losing weight for now and see if that takes away the need to transition."

- Clients needing referral letters for a medical intervention and after undergoing several sessions with a provider being told "I'm not convinced you need this/are truly transgender/ are not confused…"

- Reading on an intake summary from a previous provider that a client's "gender identity confusion is a symptom of borderline personality disorder."

- Multiple clients having to see a specific provider at a clinic in order to receive other services for an "evaluation" and being asked in depth questions about sexual history and sexual trauma history in relation to gender identity.

- Trying to refer a client for a specialized type of treatment or desired service and being told by the center or clinic, "we're not really trans-friendly/informed on trans issues/we don't talk about gender identity with our participants."

These are only a few of the hundreds of experiences that have happened as my clients try to access gender affirming care and services. Clients who are in rural areas and small towns can have great difficulty finding relevant and appropriate care within a few hours of where they live.

The book calls on us to understand that there is no one way of being gender non-conforming and that as many trans and Two Spirits that exist are as many experiences that also exist. I acknowledge that there are limitations and topics that are likely not covered well here in terms of disability rights or immigrant rights, for example. I acknowledge that there are things I am still learning and important things I may miss in this book. I know that there are similar books written by people I greatly respect. However, there are still not enough, and my hope is that someone takes the seeds of this book and expounds and writes something more creative and more comprehensive. My dream is that all of these books become regularly used as textbooks or readings in classes, internships, professional associations, study groups, and conferences.

A little, but not too much, about me

Since I was a kid, I've been asked "what are you?" and "where's your family from?" and my sibling, who has different features and darker skin, was asked "are you Black, white or mixed?" (which to the asker always meant a mix of just Black and white). Facebook recently gave me a reminder of a post I made in 2012 when I was in a grocery store and a kid pointed at me and yelled "Mom, that's not a boy, so why is it hairy?" I guess in a lot of ways my identities have made me confusing to people and sometimes frustrating because I'm not immediately "knowable." People have had many varying opinions about how I should label my identities and for a long time in my life I went along with others' beliefs. I can also be someone who people glance at and think they know many things about me based on assumptions of what categories I fit into in that particular person's worldview. People can feel frustrated if they find out that their assumption was incorrect, or if my own understanding of my identity has changed or expanded with new information and new realization. This has given me lots of headaches, heartaches, and also privileges depending on the situation. Sometimes even the very places and people I come from can be mis-informed about their own history, their own identities and what those things mean politically and spiritually. We all have many things to unlearn (or, in some cases, to re-learn what ancestors knew centuries ago). We have to untangle messaging and emotions and teachings and all kinds of things and it can look messy.

My personal journey to understanding my full self started in childhood, had a peak in my teens years, was muffled in a lot of ways through my young adulthood, and peaked again in my early thirties and continues as I reach 40. As I've gotten older I've been able to understand events, family dynamics stemming from trauma and secrets, told and untold histories, my own feelings, through a very different lens (anti-glare, non-scratch) that's given clarity on the why and who of so many parts of my self and identity that felt like looking through a blurry glass at various points in my life.

Over the years, as I've gotten to know other trans people and Two Spirits, I've seen the prism of our light. I've heard a range of our opinions, beliefs, spiritual practices, day-to-day experiences, and while we can fight each other tooth and nail sometimes (*skoden*), we also warrior up to protect each other, including our kindred who fight and pray from computers and couches, from kitchens, from street corners, from gardens, from classrooms, with cedar and tobacco smoke, with dance, and with magic.

Over the past decade, I've worked as a therapist primarily with TGNC2S people of all ages. I came out myself while I was in private therapy practice. I've had the opportunity to conduct trainings for other providers, including co-trainings and supporting trans identified presenters in developing and delivering their first workshops.

Starting point

I would recommend taking a look at the Glossary of Terms before starting to read to familiarize yourself with acronyms or terms that I may use. Please note that there is never 100 percent consensus on terminology. Language changes over time and is created by communities. These are some terms that I feel most comfortable with in 2019. I realize it may be confusing to hear different opinions on terms from various TGNC2S people. For example, "trans-sexual" is a term that most find offensive, however, I have had clients who self-identified with that term. Good practice is to use whatever language someone uses for themselves. And I also try to ensure that my clients are exposed to a range of terminology since I have had a number of people coming in and saying they've never been part of trans communities or known another trans person and feel that "all of these words and expressions are new to me."

When I use the word "transition" in the book, know that I may be speaking of any number of things a person might do in order to be more aligned with their felt gender. The first step is an awareness of not feeling content in one's assigned sex at birth in some way and starting to ask the questions: "What does this mean for me? What is going to feel better to me and what steps would I need to take for those things to happen?" Know that addressing these internal questions often means coming up against the shame and negative messaging society has surrounded us with regarding rigid gender identity and expression. Other challenges in answering these questions involve factors like survival, safety, employment, family or other relationships, and how all of these might change.

My hope is that understanding of transition is shifting away from being solely about medical interventions to be more about a range of activities or process someone might engage in, such as:

- telling people about their innate gender

- trying out terms to describe their gender to others

- asking others to use certain pronouns

- seeking a legal name change or asking school or work to use a new name on nametags and rosters

- outwardly expressing gender in ways such as clothing, hairstyle, accessories, and so on.

Not everyone has access to gender affirming medical interventions, and not every trans person wants medical interventions, for a number of reasons that could be related to cultural or spiritual beliefs, safety or social concerns, feeling that current medical options would not accurately address that person's specific dysphoria or desired gender presentation, for a few examples. People with non-binary gender identities may desire medical intervention in ways that differ from binary trans people. For instance, some may want chest masculinization surgery without nipples or "breast reduction" rather than "masculinization," some may want body sculpting procedures, facial surgery, or hair transplant only, some may want genitalia that is not a typical "penis" or "vagina." Non-binary people may face additional challenges in trying to access any of these types of interventions, as well as more traditional medical interventions for which surgeons or prescribers may require binary language and expression to consider "medically necessary." I have even known non-binary people to have difficulty proving they were "trans enough" to receive a medical procedure from a transgender health center. As I've had more and more health problems in the past few years, I've experienced more fear at going to new providers and trying to decide whether to try to explain my gender identity and expression and questioning what might happen if I do so. Or I've had the experience of explaining initially and then not having it ever acknowledged again by the staff.

It's also important to note before beginning this book that gender and sexuality are different aspects of identity. During trainings I give, I notice that many people are initially confused about how these things are separate. If I give an example of a transmasculine person who is partnered with a cisgender male, someone will ask: "Wouldn't it have been easier for him to 'stay a female' to date men?" This is conflating gender identity and sexual orientation and we then discuss attraction versus internal sense of gender identity. It's important for trans folx to understand these distinctions too, since these are not things most of us are taught when growing up. Sexuality can shift with transition and it helps to have awareness of what makes sexual orientation and gender different.

Gender is an identity, not a pathology. It is *not* up to a clinician, psychiatrist, or other provider to determine if someone is trans, just as it is not up to a provider to decide what someone's sexual orientation is or any other innate identity is. Providers can help someone on their path of deeper self-understanding and accessing internal strengths and social resources. Providers are facilitators and should give support along a journey.

Overview

In Chapter 1 we'll consider cultural humility and how the cisgender provider can be an accomplice in working for trans rights. We'll review ways to assess physical practice spaces and what it means to increase access and representation in the field. In Chapter 2 we'll learn to offer trauma informed care that is aware of ancestral and historical trauma. We'll read about ways to assist clients in surviving and embracing vitality. Chapter 3 will offer knowledge of aspects of transition for trans Two Spirit people in young and middle adulthood. There will be examples of some ways that people engage in cultural and spiritual practices to honor transition. Chapter 4 identifies new ways of thinking about family work where at least one family member or a partner is gender non-conforming. Chapter 5 reviews some medical transition options and financing ideas. Sexual health and family building is discussed as well. Chapter 6 examines considerations such as housing, healthcare, legal concerns, and social connection when working with trans elders. Chapter 7 is a letter to cisgender providers with requests regarding advocacy and trans leadership. Chapter 8 looks at ethical decision-making models and how those can be used in challenging moments. The Appendix is what I always wished was in any book I've read specifically speaking to the experience of being a trans provider working with trans folx. While there will be some practical tips, exercises, and concrete take-aways, in light of the political climate your clients are likely to be living in and some of the things mentioned above, this book asks more that you develop a viewpoint, a perspective, a willingness to question the ways you were trained and curiosity about the ways you were not.

I want to invite you on this journey of challenging yourself to understand who is left out of "research" that creates "evidence-based practices," who has been conducting the bulk of research in our fields and interpreting that data, as well as largely running organizations "serving" TGNC2S people and developing the standards of care, to stretch beyond typical practice and working style, and to move into a place of growth as you read this book and honestly assess where you are. My wishes are that this book could be transformative in some small way that could create a shift in your work which could deeply affect many lives. I completed the self assessment checklists in this book myself when I finished the manuscript and now know some of the areas where I need to continue growing and pushing myself. I hope you find the same.

> At times in this book I include stories or case examples to illustrate points. I am using myself or compilations of TGNC2S people I know, with identities disguised for privacy. I start some chapters with stories to illustrate points or themes in the text.

CHAPTER 1

Cultural Humility

*The Role of Cisgender Therapist
as Ally or Accomplice*

My grandfather, my mother's step-father, was an Iraqi Muslim who immigrated to the United States with his young daughter in the 1960s. During the early 2000s he became severely depressed. He listened daily to news in Arabic coming from an international radio station about the Iraq war. He spoke to his siblings there on the phone when they were able to get to a working telephone and heard about their hunger, lack of medicine in hospitals, and daily bombings of their city. He feared for the lives of all of his family in southern Iraq daily. He saw a therapist and took medication, but it didn't seem that the therapist had any awareness of the complicated political factors at play and the experiences he'd had in secretly returning to his country several times since being in the United States. There didn't seem to be an intersectional lens being used in his treatment. His religion and faith were not incorporated into his care. He ended up receiving electro-convulsive therapy, which helped the depression somewhat, but then he was diagnosed with cancer and died. While therapy would not have stopped the traumatic events happening in his homeland, I wondered if there was more culturally relevant and informed care that he could have received that would have been more effective and beneficial. I know that he felt incredibly isolated in his experiences and was exposed to hurtful political rhetoric daily and I think that his therapy could have addressed those things. This is only one personal story that illustrates the reasons that cultural humility as providers is so important. Without it, we can miss the very heart of the issues someone is coming to us with. We can be looking at "presenting problems" through our own life experience and ways of understanding and offer care in a way that does not connect with the person we are working with.

At this point, I've done a lot of training for professionals. Often people express that they want more practical skills and "how-tos." While I understand this, before we can implement skills effectively, we need to have a framework from which we're approaching our work. Without that, implementation of skills and tools can end up being ineffective or even harmful.

What is cultural humility?

The term was coined in 1998 by Melanie Tervalon and Jann Murray-Garcia in response to the idea of "cultural competence." The term and concept of cultural competence says that a person can become "competent" in a culture that is not their own. It prioritizes academic knowledge over lived experience. It gives providers the idea that taking a workshop or course can make you "competent." It also focuses on viewing people as "others" and neglects a social justice agenda (Fisher-Borne, Cain, & Martin 2015). Models promoting cultural competence can emphasize "exposure" to cultures other than one's own, versus developing an anti-racist analysis and examining one's own ethnocentric and hetero-normative stumbling blocks. A cultural humility approach calls us on to increase awareness of our own classism, ableism, transphobia, for example, and the way that these things influence our subconscious thoughts and behaviors. Another critique of cultural competence is that often "culture" is used to refer just to race or ethnicity, considers other aspects of identity as "secondary" or "not innate" to a person, and ignores intersections of identity. Cultural humility is about assuming a position in regards to the power dynamics that are held by providers, professionals, and even students with academic privilege. It's about a commitment to self-reflection, life-long learning, and awareness of the ways that problems or symptoms are expressed. It's an understanding that the types of treatment desired, and that are appropriate, are influenced by culture, identities, and lived experiences. Cultural humility recognizes that culture is not static or unchanging and that we are required as practitioners to address inequalities. There is an accountability to do our own internal work and also to demand institutional accountability in addressing inequity and power imbalances. In regards to working with TGNC2S people, it also means understanding ways in which your own views and experiences with gender are influenced by your own culture and multiple identities. These identities are linked, socially constructed, and affected by systemic inequities. Using an approach that assists clients in recognizing social oppression can be especially helpful because minorities are often socialized to internalize and blame themselves for the challenges they face (Adames & Chavez-Dueñas 2017; Parham, White, & Ajamu 1999).

Ally or accomplice

What makes a cisgender therapist an ally or accomplice to trans, Two Spirit, and gender non-conforming people? Or a white trans identified therapist an accomplice or co-conspirator with gender non-conforming clients of color?

Like the concept of cultural competence, the term "ally" has also been challenged. Mia McKenzie says,

"Currently operating in solidarity with" is undeniably an action. It describes what a person is doing in the moment. It does not give credit for past acts of solidarity without regard for current behavior. It does not assume future acts of solidarity. It speaks only to the actions of the present. (2014, p.138)

In claiming to be an "ally," we're often giving ourselves a past, present, and future identity that is not necessarily validated by the people we think we're "allied" with. We haven't earned trust by consistency. The challenge is that, with any type of privilege we hold, we can rest on that privilege. That can look like disengaging from advocacy and activism, ignoring microaggressions, getting lazy about ongoing learning and listening, also keeping ourselves in the spotlight, not highlighting other voices, sitting in all the seats, and refusing to share power. Often, you can recognize an ally because (with good intentions) they are rushing ahead of the group they are supposed to be allied with and making decisions on behalf of the group.

An example of this would be the cisgender parent of a trans youth contacting a legislator to sponsor a bill related to legal document changes, without seeking input on the language of the bill from larger trans community or finding out whether this bill would even be desired by the larger trans community. Another example, a group of cisgender providers approaching a governing body (either local government or professional boards) to inform them of issues affecting trans individuals, rather than approaching the same body to insist that they meet with trans individuals to hear directly about the issues of concern. A third example, that cisgender providers create a "resource list" for trans folx, listing their own services and that of providers they trust and are friends with, versus asking how to amplify and share the same type of lists that have been created by trans folx, reviewing and recommending area providers. You might also see LGBTQ+ organizations with no people of color in leadership or transgender-focused organizations with no trans people on staff or in leadership. You might see white donors wanting to start their own foundations to benefit LGBTQ+ people instead of just donating their funds to trans-led organizations that center people of color.

What makes an accomplice or co-conspirator?

If we think about what those words mean, they imply a shared risk, shared weight of responsibility. "The thing I don't like about the word ally is that it is so wrought with guilt and shame and grief that it prevents people from doing what they ought to do," says Alicia Garza (Move to End Violence 2016). "To be a comrade is to be fierce and to take action to upend the status quo… I would be willing to risk social standing, ambition, and acceptance by my peers to do the right thing" (Karen Tronsgard-Scott, in Move to End Violence 2016).

If allyship often looks like expressing empathy, support, doing advocacy or activism things publicly to alleviate feelings of guilt or complicity, then an accomplice, comrade, or co-conspirator looks like someone who's rolled up their sleeves to get down and dirty, behind the scenes a lot of times, in working to challenge big systems and business as usual, in ways that can come with personal risk. Doesn't sound as cozy and nice as ally-land does it? There are a lot of ways to be an accomplice in many different settings. Yes, folks argue and have strong opinions about how you need to do it. I don't think an either/or, extreme opinion is helpful most of the time. The point is that we need to get real with ourselves and seriously reflect on how to move past being an "ally" to an accomplice or co-conspirator.

How can I implement this idea?

We often start where we are. What systems are you part of? Do you work in an organization or agency, participate in the insurance healthcare system, exist in a school/academic system or faith group, work in a specific neighborhood with housing policies and practices, service delivery needs, and so on? How can you challenge inequity, discrimination, and oppression in those places? How has fear or complacency been holding you back from doing so and what is the first step you can take in spite of your emotions?

Increasing access, increasing equity

Consider the physical space where you work. How would a gender non-conforming person of color who enters that space know that they were in an affirming place? What's absent or present now that doesn't make this the case? Consider visuals (artwork, reading material laying around, signs), verbal cues (greetings by various staff, language used), forms (phrasing, language, culturally relevant terms), access to necessities such as all gender, Americans with Disabilities Act (ADA) accessible restrooms or lodgings, for example. What do you need to change or advocate to change in order for that to happen? What privileges do you have to leverage for these changes and what risk will you take on?

Consider the policies. Is there a non-discrimination policy that includes gender identity and expression? Is the healthcare policy offered one that covers trans healthcare?

Contemplate the ways you can advocate for justice outside of your paid employment or internship. What steps can you take to make things better for those who hold the most marginalized identities? We know that when things get better for folks facing the most discrimination, then everybody will be better off.

We need to evaluate the curriculum in the schools that are educating those of us in healing, healthcare, and "helping" professions. How can you request or demand anti-racist and trans affirming curriculum in the school you attend or attended? In your professional associations? We need to insist on developing anti-racist and trans affirming policies and environments in the programs that are granting professional degrees and licenses.

In terms of creating more access in the field for gender non-conforming people:

- Can you recruit gender non-conforming interns at your site?

- Can you provide free clinical supervision for a trans clinician seeking licensure?

- Can you sponsor or provide funding for trans identified providers to attend conferences or continuing education classes that are required for licensure?

- Where in your workplace can you hire or advocate for hiring trans, Two Spirit, and GNC individuals (including adjusting "job requirements/qualifications" to allow for hiring folks with lived experience who can be trained and mentored without a degree)?

- How do you ensure that your workplace views this as a priority in terms of representation? Do you hire TGNC2S staff at the front desk? To answer phones? As community liaisons or peer mentors? As graphic designers or social media marketers? As accountants, grant writers, and supervisors?

One thing I often encourage groups of cisgender clinicians and providers in medical or community organizations to do is to pass along training requests or panel requests they get to TGNC2S providers or community members, or to ask to co-train and give equal pay to the TGNC2S person, to ask legislators who want to meet with their professional association to meet with the local trans rights group instead, to basically do whatever possible to use privilege to ensure that queer/trans Black, Indigenous people of color (QTBIPOC) are "at the table" and have decision-making power.

When building your referral network, how are you seeking culturally relevant resources for your clients? What relationships have you formed that can assist with this? What time have you committed to putting these resources together for your clients? How do you know the demographics of in-person or online support groups you're referring to? Working with gender non-conforming people, especially people of color, requires different referral sources than you may use for cisgender, heterosexual, white clients.

Some examples of community resources I've been able to refer and connect clients with over the years:

- Black trans therapy group

- Black trans women support group

- POC trans affirming Christian church

- QTPOC camping trip group

- queer/trans affirming and led Jewish schtiebel

- Two Spirit annual gatherings

- coalition for trans Latinas

- inclusive outdoor and climbing groups for Natives

- POC trans inclusive drag performance groups

- queer/trans Black barbers and stylists

- Latinx Pride festival

- queer POC herbalists

- POC trans affirming energy healers

- gender non-conforming Black physicians

- BIPOC tarot readers

- QTPOC-led summer camp

- QTPOC community gardening projects

- trans Muslim networks

- TPOC political organizing groups.

CASE EXAMPLE

As a therapist in a small community, it was difficult to find my own trusted therapist who wasn't someone I was friends with or sharing office space with. I'd heard of a therapist who was supposedly "trans friendly" and did a type of trauma work I wanted to do to address some long-standing trauma. Her office was very "neutral." No images of people anywhere, no reading materials, just waiting room chairs and either blank walls or some light-colored paintings maybe. Nothing that would put me at ease. I talked about my gender identity at first and she said she understood so we started the trauma work. Unfortunately, after several sessions, she was still mis-gendering me at the end of session or to other people in the waiting room, even after some corrections. I did feel like the trauma work had helped me have some healing, but I reached a point where the mis-gendering was becoming so annoying and uncomfortable that I decided it wasn't beneficial to me to continue. I probably should have explained to her honestly why I was ending, but just didn't have the emotional energy at the time.

CASE EXAMPLE

I'm sitting across from a mixed race trans client who previously received low cost counseling services from a group advertising as LGBTQ+ friendly or trans-friendly. Like many others, my client found that "friendly" doesn't necessarily mean aware or informed, even if there are some other shared identities. The therapist used inappropriate language in trying to talk about the client's gender and sexual identities and lost the trust of the client from the start. They wanted to be somewhere where they felt more comfortable talking about racial identity, experiences of racism, and challenges related to being a gender non-conforming femme. They wanted to come to therapy as their whole self, not needing to compartmentalize in order to participate in counseling.

CASE EXAMPLE

A therapist consulted with me about one of his cases. His client was a trans Latina immigrant who had received orchiectomy surgery and had a complication. She was fearful and angry and was seeking help with the complication from the hospital, but the hospital was not taking responsibility or wanting to be further involved, stating that she must not have followed their recovery instructions properly. Upon further discussion it became clear that the hospital had not offered translation services during any of their meetings with the patient prior to the surgery. While his client does speak English, it is not her first language and all written materials and forms were provided only in English. The clinician requested a meeting with hospital staff to discuss the concerns but the meeting was not granted. The clinician discussed the client's options with her in terms of filing a complaint and requesting translation at a meeting with the surgeon and his staff, or seeking out consultation and revision with another surgeon. The clinician also acknowledged the traumatic experiences this client was going through in trying to manage an upsetting complication while not receiving help from the place that performed her surgery. The client did not feel able to address that traumatic aspect until the complication was addressed. The client chose to move on and find a new surgeon. The clinician reached out to another surgeon in the area, spoke about the need for interpreter services and Spanish handouts, and asked if the surgeon felt that he could potentially resolve this particular complication. He did, met with the patient who was able to ask questions with interpreter services present, and they collaborated on a plan for healing and then revision surgery.

CASE EXAMPLE

A Native friend had been trying for some time to find therapy services that were free or low cost, had ADA accessible facilities, and would be culturally sensitive to a Native Two Spirit. After several months search, they were excited to find an agency that said it met this criteria. They arrived in the lobby and found that the therapist they were supposed to see had a poster of a sports team with a racist (anti-Native) mascot on the outside of his office door. My friend just turned around and left, because any agency that doesn't understand how these mascots are hurtful to Native people cannot offer culturally sensitive care.

SELF ASSESSMENT

1. I check in with myself periodically to ask whether I am assuming "competence" or taking a position of humility.

   Y   N

2. In the past year, I have invested time and effort into learning about at least one identity or culture that I do not share.

   Y   N

3. In the past year, I have assessed what TGNC2S may experience when present in my facility, organization, program, etc.

   Y   N

4. I have advocated for changes at my place of education or employment to ensure a more trans affirming experience for clients/patients, as well as providers/employees.

   Y   N

5. In my current position, I do things that may be uncomfortable, risky, scary, or inconvenient in striving to increase access for TGNC2S people in the healing, healthcare, "helping" fields.

   Y   N

6. I am willing to relinquish my position on a board, committee, paid staff, and so on, so that there can be more TGNC2S representation. I am willing to request that TGNC2S people be recruited for these positions, especially POC.

   Y   N

7. I have participated in some form of advocacy for trans rights.

   Y   N

8. I have a holistic, culturally representative referral network.

   Y   N

Trauma Informed Care that Acknowledges Ancestral Trauma and Survivance/Resilience

What is systemic or structural oppression?

Society includes institutions such as schools, faith centers, governmental bodies and agencies, medical centers, businesses and places of employment, detention and prison systems, judicial and court systems, as well as cultural practices, beliefs, traditions, and ideologies. The majority of these systems and institutions operate hierarchically, which generally means that historically dominant and privileged groups maintain higher and more desirable positions, positions of power, and positions of assumed innocence versus being assumed guilty until proof of innocence. The current status quo maintains systems that are classist, racist, ableist, xenophobic, transphobic, and homophobic in nature. The way that systems operate often uphold power for those who are privileged and continue to prevent people with oppressed identities from participating and benefiting. Individuals within those systems may be unaware of their own biases and take their privileges for granted. People can, and often do, belong to one group that is marginalized or targeted and another group that holds power and privilege. People can hold multiple identities that are discriminated against and oppressed.

Regular experiences of oppression and how they create a trauma response

Imagine that there is a 16-year-old Black woman of trans experience living in a medium sized town, in a working class home, attending public high school. She is harassed and threatened at school daily by peers due to her gender presentation. Eventually she begins to defend herself physically against the harassment and receives multiple school suspensions. She runs away from home in anger and hurt one day and winds up in juvenile detention with a probation officer. This is while many middle class white youth in her town often run away overnight and are simply returned home by the police who pick them up. Her mother supports her gender identity, but her probation officer doesn't and won't advocate for her within the juvenile court and detention systems. Because of the racism experienced historically by Black youth and Black women, her mother fears that her gender expression will make her even more of a target. Because of her age, she is told in various settings that she doesn't know who she is yet and can't make decisions about what is right for her body and spirit. This young person is daily experiencing oppression related to race, gender, age, and class. What is the emotional impact on someone in this situation, involved in these systems, who is simply not allowed to just attend school and be herself? This is after she struggled in childhood to express herself despite the judgment and punishment of adults in her environment. What type of trauma response comes with living in fear of physical or sexual assault on a daily basis? What trauma comes with knowing that your ancestors were subjected to the same fears? The systems and culture expect the young person to mold to their requirements, expectations, and norms. If she doesn't or can't, she is punished.

Imagine that there is a 60-year-old white transmasculine person who has not been able to stay on HRT for various reasons, who is hard of hearing, and has an autoimmune disorder that creates frequent periods of illness. This person lives in a rural area with no support from family of origin and his adult children refuse to speak to him. He has only been able to find part time employment and has to navigate medical care often. He has to choose between trying to educate resistant medical staff about his identity and body, or allowing himself to be gendered however others choose, and overhearing jokes and negative comments about his body by receptionists and nurses. There are no LGBTQ+ centers or transgender support where he lives. He has found some online groups but most of the members are much younger than he is. He fears for his safety as he ages and wonders who will take care of him when he is unable to live alone. What experiences of oppression does this person have on a regular basis? In what ways are the systems he has to navigate created to erase him, to humiliate him, to choose not to serve him appropriately? What would the emotional toll of this regular experience be?

Imagine that there is a 28-year-old gender non-conforming person whose father is a Muslim Palestinian immigrant and whose mother died when this person was a young child. The young adult attended college where they started to more fully understand their gender and identity. While in college they encountered anti-Muslim, anti-Arab attitudes from classmates at times, though they were also part of a campus Arab student union and cultural center. They are working on negotiating their relationship to their gender in relation to their Muslim identity. The relationships with their father, religion, Arab American identity are all important to this person. Anti-Arab, Anti-Muslim sentiment and violence in the West creates ongoing real safety concerns for this person and their loved ones. They are also navigating the job market, trying to predict how their last name might impact ability to receive interviews or offers, as well as how or whether to discuss their gender identity with employers. How would daily fears of physical attack impact this person? In what ways are various systems and culture interacting in oppressive ways towards this person?

How do we recognize ancestral or intergenerational trauma?

Sometimes called "historical trauma," the concept of ancestral or intergenerational trauma was initially developed in the 1980s by First Nations and Aboriginal peoples in Canada to explain the seeming unending cycle of trauma and despair among Indigenous communities (Wesley-Esquimaux & Smolewski 2004). Essentially, when the enormous trauma of genocide, forced removal from ancestral land, separation of families, and loss of culture occurs, the wounds of these experiences are passed down and inherited. Indigenous scholar Vera Martin called it "blood memory" and, in referencing her work, Gregory Phillips said "It is a collective memory of what has happened and what has not happened" (2008). Ways in which genocide was carried out include offering rewards for the hunting and killing/extermination of tribal people, stealing tribal lands and forcing people onto reservations, destroying the natural food source of Indigenous peoples, encouraging intermarriage of whites and rape in an attempt to eradicate the blood of the group, placing children in boarding schools and adopting Native children away from their tribe into white families, and encouraging the assimilation into white culture of the group so that they must abandon or hide cultural practices and identifiers in order to survive. At the same time as enacting these traumas, the dominant group was also introducing alcohol use and encouraging intoxication. In addition, oppression and discrimination of Indigenous peoples is still occurring, so the ancestral trauma mingles with present day trauma. Even family members who do not have direct experience of the trauma itself can feel the effects generations later (Walters *et al.* 2011).

The effects of using enslaved Black people to build global capitalism and the US economy are similar.

The experiences of the dreaded slave ship dungeons of the Middle Passage—in which millions of souls still rest at the bottom of the Atlantic—the auction blocks, the rapes, whippings and lynchings, the slave patrols, the backbreaking and life-ending labor at gunpoint, the separation of families all inflicted psychological damage on the victims and their descendants. (Love 2016)

Dr. Joy DeGruy defined this as "post-traumatic slave syndrome" in her 2017 book with the same title. Research has also shown that trauma can alter DNA gene expression, so that trauma is literally inherited from ancestors (CBC News 2015). "I think we as a culture need to make some major changes in the way we think about harm caused by historical trauma," said Dr. Monnica Williams. "We now know it's not simply 'in the past' but continues to influence descendants through both social and genetic (epigenetic) mechanisms" (Love 2016). And again, Black folx continue to experience oppression and discrimination from systems and structures (as well as individuals), so intergenerational trauma compounds with present trauma.

You may see demonstrations of the effects of this type of trauma through self injurious behaviors, depression, suicidal ideation, anxiety, substance abuse, anger and violent behavior, dissociation, emotional numbing, hypervigilance, difficulty with attachment between parents and children, internalized oppression and identification with dominant culture's view of own identity, leading to self hatred or low self esteem, and so on. "I think you're dealing with generations of people who have been damaged by colonialism," Dr. Cornelia Wieman says, "and the way that we have been treated by the dominant culture makes you feel dispirited. You feel devalued and so people will turn to things like addictions as a way of coping, of self-medicating, of not really wanting to be here because their situation is just so intolerable" (in Wadden 2006). You might also see physical illness and chronic pain: "A significant proportion of Native people are struggling with health disparities that stem from intergenerational trauma" (Dr. Maria Yellow Horse Brave Heart, in Brave Heart *et al.* 2011). To make things worse, the dominant group and culture is aware of these effects of ancestral, historical, and intergenerational trauma, and uses them to further disenfranchise and blame that group of people. "The sign of ultimate oppression working is when the oppressor can take away his hands, stand back and say 'look at what they're doing to themselves'" (Gourneau 2015).

How can we adapt treatment models to allow for cultural relevance?

It is important to recognize that there is limited evidence that trauma treatments developed in the West are effective across cultures. In the first assessment with a client, a therapist will want to ask about cultural identity and experiences, spiritual beliefs and practices, any complementary treatment desired, such as working with other types of healers, participating in rituals, using culturally specific medicine or remedies, relationship structures, and decision-making processes. The therapist must then prioritize time outside of sessions to learn about the norms, values, beliefs, behaviors, and needs of the client's culture. Therapists should also take care not to assume that two people from the same culture have the same experiences or interpretations of events. Another consideration is that trauma symptoms, the way they are described, outwardly expressed, and the perceived cause or meaning of the symptoms can be culture specific. If, after assessment, the therapist chooses to use a Western-developed therapy treatment, it should not minimize, or interfere with, culturally traditional healing practices.

One trauma treatment is EMDR (eye movement desensitization and re-processing) therapy. In order to provide relevant EMDR, a practitioner must: adapt EMDR methods to a client's cultural context and empower clients to be culturally aware (which requires first learning about the client's culture, then using creativity), as appropriate, and implement EMDR interventions that treat the internalized effects of culturally based trauma (Nickerson 2017). One important adaptation might be that the negative beliefs about self that are addressed are specifically caused by systemic oppression and the goal is to reduce internalized oppression.

Other ways that treatments such as dialectical behavior therapy

(DBT) and somatic experiencing (SE) have been adapted include holding identity-based group treatments, re-naming key concepts and skills to culturally relevant names and concepts, and utilizing cultural historical examples of triumph or struggle in the face of hardship as internal resourcing and resilience strategies. One example is a trans and gender non-conforming SE group (Briggs, Hayes, & Changaris 2018).

At times, it will be necessary to partner with a local cultural group in providing relevant, trauma informed care, as in the example of psychologists partnering with an Indigenous program and healing lodge to assist clients in a community in addressing the effects of historical trauma (Gone 2009).

What about survivance and resilience?

Anishinaabe writer and critic, Gerald Vizenor, promoted the term "survivance" in 1994, to refer not just to survival, but to an "active presence." The concept of survivance rejects the colonial narrative of Native as victim or Native as absent or past tense—those "poor Indians" or those "Indians that used to be here" (2008). Vizenor says that survivance is a joining of survival, resistance, and presence, that often looks like creation, story-telling, sense of place, vision, and ongoing process. In fact, the therapist's idea of what "healing" or "trauma recovery" looks like may need to be questioned. For example: "Throughout his writings, Vizenor describes the trickster as a force who heals and balances the world. The trickster does not unify, does not resolve and remove contradiction, fragmentation or multiplicities. He holds them in balance" (Madsen 2008, pp.67–68). Survivance and healing from cultural or historical trauma may not look like assimilation into the dominant culture or a clean resolution, or what the therapist views as positive social outcomes.

The word resilience is commonly defined as: to recover from difficulty, to adjust to change, to bounce back from adversity. We likely will need to expand our understanding of this word as well.

How can we assist clients in building resilience?

First, we recognize that trans, Two Spirit, and gender non-conforming folx are already incredibly resilient. Simply existing in the face of enormous challenge and even oppression is resilient and strong. TGNC2S people are creative and resourceful. Highlighting this fact, as well as the gifts and skills your client already has, is the place to start. Sometimes a client might need you to help them see the specific ways they are resilient.

Research has shown various types of resilience in gender non-conforming individuals. Some of these are defining oneself in a validating way, recognizing that understanding of self can shift, embracing self worth, awareness of oppression, connection with a supportive community, cultivating hope for the future, social activism, and being a positive role model for others (Singh, Hays, & Watson 2011; Singh & McElroy 2011).

As providers, we can assist clients in engaging in each of those resilience strategies, including assisting with connection to a broader supportive community and finding ways to participate in creating social change.

A qualitative study of LGBTQ+ youth (Asakura 2016) emphasizes that resilience is not necessarily about overcoming a challenge or reaching a turning point, but existing despite pain. Being resilient and LGBTQ+ means that youth continue to "show up every day," are "able to get out of bed," and have "hope for the future," knowing that they must continue to struggle to exist within their lived realities. We also recognize context-dependent resilience. What we typically think of as "positive" outcomes, or what we mean when we say someone is "doing well," can look different for TGNC2S individuals, especially those with multiple marginalized identities. Young people in the study rejected the normative definitions of positive adaptation, such as the absence of psychopathologies and school success. As evidenced by the choice of phrases such as "still struggling," "battling through," "still fighting," and having "your head above water," youth emphasized the experience of pain as the courageous aspect of continuing to move through adversities. As providers, we can acknowledge our clients' resourcefulness and survival in the midst of hetero-cis-normative systems.

As mentioned earlier, resilience may take the form of social activism. TGNC2S folks may choose to engage in activist work and community organizing to address various oppressions, shift cultural norms, create resources, and bring about social change. It is important to see that this work can be healing. I've heard therapists in the past make statements about TGNC2S clients who were activists such as "I don't know if he can really emotionally handle this kind of thing," "they'll burn out doing that work," "why would she knowingly put herself in the middle of a dangerous situation, as if she doesn't have enough trauma already?," and so on. While most likely the providers were speaking from a place of concern for their clients, they were missing potentially powerful and transformative effects of engaging in activism. For example, a study on community resilience in environmental activism identified sovereignty or self reliance, sustainability, community relational bonds, and direct community member participation as benefits (Case 2016).

What is community care and how do I help clients with that?

People experiencing oppression often realize that institutions are not open to providing care for them, are not educated in how to provide care, or that certain resources simply don't exist. Some (definitely not all) of the ways that I've seen trans folx care for each other include fundraising online or with events or rent parties to help each other pay bills, find housing, achieve medical care, pay bail, or bridge gaps between employment; feeding each other by cooking meals, dropping off groceries, bringing leftovers from a restaurant job, passing along a grubhub card or meal delivery kit's free meal offer; taking care of each other after surgeries, giving rides to appointments and jobs or community events, sharing medication when it is needed but can't be accessed; sharing information about trans-friendly providers and resources; sharing information about sexual health practices and legal support; sending out community alarms when someone is being harassed in a public area or is missing; offering emotional support and validation to counter all the invalidation and discrimination being experienced; serving as crisis support teams when someone feels suicidal; creating space together on holidays when most people are with biological family; coming over to spend time with the child of another trans person who needs a nap or a break from parenting; swapping clothing; teaching make-up skills; creating organizations and networks to increase access to all types of support and services; and more!

While it shouldn't just be up to QTBIPOC folx to take care of themselves and their needs, the examples I listed are reasons that it can be powerful for a trans person to experience community. Even if the only access to community is online, that community can still care for its members in various ways. Providers should help clients locate TGNC2S spaces and community online or in person.

Reyna is a Filipinx transmasculine client who uses she/her pronouns. She is studying race and equity in college. She expresses a lot of difficulty connecting to other people, she struggles with substance abuse, and reports having nightmares frequently. She shares experiences of racism and transphobia she went through during high school. She states that she is not in contact with any Filipinx community, though her friend group is mostly people of color of various ethnicities. She says that growing up she did not learn much of her heritage or cultural practices and beliefs from her mother. She does not know much of Filipinx history. She described this as "feeling white but being related to in the world as POC."

One of the first steps I took was to connect her with a local Asian Solidarity activism group. Then I began to ask her to learn about Filipinx history and spiritualities. She started to be excited by what she was learning and we would discuss these things and how they affected her. We discussed that she was made of her ancestors' blood and DNA. We processed grief that she felt as she learned of things her ancestors went through due to colonization, as well as her attempt to emotionally reconcile living in a country that was heavily involved in that colonization over time. She began to have conversations with her mother about her mother's experiences and stories from other relatives in the Philippines. She was able to learn the reasons her mother had not shared these things with her when she was growing up and her mother apologized for not doing this. Reyna recognized the strength and power she had inherited through her ancestral line. We processed experiences of racism she goes through regularly and how she wanted to handle those things in the moment. Reyna began to feel that she could start to engage in advocacy for Filipinx rights and made a friend in the Asian Solidarity group. Her nightmares decreased and so did her substance abuse. She stated that she was engaging in healing ancestral trauma, that she believed her line was waiting on someone like her to be able to do this spiritual work, and that she was feeling more secure in all her identities.

SELF ASSESSMENT

1. I am able to identify the institutions that affect my clients' daily lives.

   Y   N

2. I am able to identify the ways that structures and systems marginalize and oppress my clients.

   Y   N

3. I have a working understanding of ancestral/historical/intergenerational trauma.

   Y   N

4. I have ideas about how to recognize internalized oppression and to talk about it with clients.

   Y   N

5. I have ideas about ways to adapt treatments to be culturally relevant or of various local cultural groups to partner with.

   Y   N

6. I know how to recognize survivance and resilience in many forms in my clients.

   Y   N

7. I have thoughts about how to go about connecting clients to various resilience strategies and trans or Two Spirit community.

   Y   N

Scenarios

You are seeing a Senegalese 30 year old, transfeminine client who is seeking help with gender transition. This client lives in a small town in a rural area. She is not "out" to anyone yet and due to earning a low wage, she lives with her mother and uncle and borrows her mother's car to get to work. She does not have access to the car much outside of going to work. Her current health insurance through her job does not cover trans healthcare and the list of "in-network" providers she can see for medical and mental healthcare is pretty much useless in enabling her to access care as the list is small and many providers say they actually don't accept the insurance when she calls. She does not have any gender non-conforming friends other than knowing that some people in an online D&D game that she plays are transgender. She has known she was trans for years but felt hopeless to live as herself. She knows her uncle would not be supportive and likely would be hostile and she is unsure of how her mother would react to learning she is transgender.

What would be the first thing you would focus on with this client? Why?

. . . .

. . . .

. . . .

. . . .

. . . .

. . . .

. . . .

. . . .

. . . .

. . . .

What else would you want to learn about the client?

. . . .

. . . .

. . . .

. . . .

. . . .

. . . .

. . . .

. . . .

. . . .

What resources and groups in the area would you make contact with?

. . . .

. . . .

. . . .

. . . .

. . . .

. . . .

. . . .

. . . .

. . . .

. . . .

Given that this person currently lives in a rural area with few resources, what else would you explore to assist her in expanding a support network and meeting basic needs?

. . . .

. . . .

. . . .

. . . .

. . . .

. . . .

. . . .

. . . .

. . . .

. . . .

CHAPTER 3

Transition for Trans and Two Spirit Young and Middle Adults

Identity formation

I want to tell you a story. There was a little kid, assigned female at birth, who asked to "be a man" for Halloween at age three. And felt really good knocking on doors as the sky turned orange, then black, waiting for the sound of a piece of candy plopping into a plastic bucket, until they realized that adults were asking "Who are you?" There was a pause and they saw that they were supposed to be a *specific* man, so doing some quick thinking, they started answering with the first thing that came to mind, "Mr. Baloneyhead." This kid loved wearing bright dresses with shiny shoes and also the tuxedo they somehow convinced a grandmother to buy for them one year. They showed up to their first middle school dance in a basketball uniform and high tops, feeling like they looked so fine but quickly realized that wasn't the "right" thing and the next year wore a dress. They went through school years as a girl, not knowing there was such a thing as "gender non-conforming" or "cisgender" or "transgender" or "Two Spirit" or "genderqueer" or "gender fluid." Not knowing there were expressions like "femme," "stud," "masc," "butch," and more. There was no internet. The local library had no books about any of these things as far as the young person could tell and nobody ever mentioned anything like it. Except that time in high school when they and a friend were minding their own business and some angry grown men surrounded their friend, demanding that the teenager "prove" whether they were a boy or girl. Through young adult years their gender expression ranged from somewhat masculine to femme. And they felt pretty comfortable alone with all of it. It was other people's reactions that caused discomfort. They finally decided to publicly embrace their sexuality, which did lead to being cut off from most biological family, creating a wound that will never fully close. In their early thirties, after existing for that long as a woman, they had learned about multiple genders and knew that they weren't cisgender and this explained how they'd felt all these years. These various discoveries and understandings have complicated relationships and knowledge of how to be in community at times. They're still on a journey of finding ways to express their gender that feel good, ways to talk about it that feel good, understanding what feels bad, and so on. You got it, Mr. Baloneyhead is me. And, now, I realize that all my identities are a gift.

A lot of times I encounter a belief that "real" gender non-conforming people have understood and expressed their gender outwardly since an early age. If someone is starting to outwardly express a gender non-conforming identity in adulthood, sometimes people around them are skeptical or doubt the authenticity of that identity. This is based on misunderstanding of gender as well as the power of socialization and cultural pressure.

There are strong messages about gender all around us and these start even before a baby is born, in most cases. Whether we think we do or not, we often have assumptions and beliefs about what it is to be "girl," "boy," "man," "woman." At this point in time, other genders are not reflected in the mainstream sufficiently to be included in those assumptions and stereotypes. Even families who attempt to be "neutral" in how they raise kids related to gender are likely acting in ways that are unintentionally reinforcing gender stereotypes. Or at least are not a strong enough "neutral" space to counterbalance all the other gender messaging going on in their kids' worlds.

This messaging shows up daily in a million ways. My partner recently worked for a while teaching science in Head Start classes. Regularly kids would ask them "Are you a boy or a girl?" One asked "Why do you have short hair? I'm a boy and I have short hair." During an activity where the class pretended to be flowers and grow, if a boy said he was a pink flower inevitably other kids would immediately say "You can't be pink. Boys aren't pink." A friend recently told me a story of a young boy being given a purple bike and having a meltdown, yelling "I'm not a f***, purple is for f***s!"

A lot of parents have said to me, "I never steered her towards pink or girly things. I would have let her play with any kind of toys. So I don't know how she ended up being so into princesses and dolls, I guess girls really are just wired a certain way!" Well, if we consider the strong gender boxes kids in preschool are already keeping each other in based on the social representation they see, based on behaviors they observe, shouldn't it surprise us *more* when a child is able to bring themselves to express who they are despite their friends making fun of them, despite being called names or having other kids not want to play with them? And, in a lot of cases, despite being punished for that at home and told it's wrong? Or being steered away from certain things in more subtle ways by parents, such as when I overheard a parent telling their young son who wanted some lipstick that lipstick wasn't "healthy" and could "make you sick." This wise child said "Well, I better tell my teacher it's not safe because she wears it."

There's also the fact that many religious and cultural practices have specific gender roles. Who does what activity or holds what position or is valued in a certain way is related to gender. Can you imagine being a young person who wants to be involved in your religious community, who wants to participate in cultural traditions and learn from elders, and knowing that this means adhering to the prescribed and expected gender identity and roles? Can you imagine the fear of losing all of those extremely important things in order to express your gender in the way that feels true to you?

It's also the case that most young people since the late 1800s have not grown up with many examples of multiple gender identities or people who were gender non-conforming. This is because European settlers and Christian missionaries had murdered many Two Spirits or placed them in boarding schools to be "reformed." They were forced to wear clothing and take on roles associated with their assigned gender (Brayboy 2017; Hunt 2016). Any African brought to Turtle Island for slavery would have had to hide any gender diversity and conform to the same gender expressions and roles under threat of death or punishment by slave-owners. Through separation and punishment, combined with missionary efforts, many tribal peoples lost traditional knowledge. When young people did know of gender variance, it was often talked about negatively or avoided as a topic. I've talked to so many adults who came out in their late twenties to late sixties, who said "I just didn't know this was an option. I didn't know about other genders," or "There was one person in the community I knew was gender non-conforming and it was something you did *not* want to be."

I've noticed it's also hard for some people to accept that gender can be fluid. Some people experience changes in their gender, whether over short periods of time such as day to day or over longer periods, where they may express and experience a gender identity for a period, then that changes later on, and maybe changes again. These are not changes that can be imposed from the outside, from someone else (meaning you can't change your felt gender because someone else wants you to), rather they are the internal truths of that person. For the health of our society, we need to be able to allow our understandings of someone to shift, to change, if that's what the person communicates to us.

Cultural relevance in referral and education for individuals and families

Your clients may need support that is relevant to their own spirituality, racial and ethnic identity, cultural traditions, and more. No provider can be everything to each and every client. In order to offer good care, we need to have referral networks, resources, and information for a client's particular needs. If we're in a location or role that doesn't already have these networks and resources in place, we will need to spend time creating them. This could entail building relationships with local organizations or community members, identifying good online resources, purchasing a variety of books to loan to clients, and creating a resource list that is varied and extensive in nature. If there is a gap in resources in your area, can you ask a particular spiritual leader or faith group about meeting that need? Do you have a relationship with multiple trans affirming or trans identified faith leaders or spiritual healers you can connect clients with? Have your own resource lists been "vetted" by trans, 2S, GNC folx?

One group of researchers stated that for a therapist to develop a strong working relationship and conduct effective counseling with a client who is culturally different [from the therapist], the therapist must be able to overcome the natural tendency to view one's own beliefs, values, and worldview as superior, and instead be open to the beliefs, values, and worldview of the diverse client (Hook *et al.* 2013, p.2).

I would add that, in addition to openness, there must be an active learning, a willingness to take the steps to find out what an identity or experience means to your particular client—not to a group or people who share an identity, but to that person in their context.

In my practice, I've found it helpful with some clients and families to be able to share stories and information about the long history of multiple genders around the world. The Ashtime of the Maale of Ethiopia, Moshoga in Kenya, Waria of Indonesia, Muxe in the Zapotec culture of Mexico, Khanith of parts of the Arabian peninsula, "sworn virgins" in the Balkans, and "uranians" of England, are only a few examples of historical traditional gender identities and roles that are beyond just "male" and "female." There are many African spiritual beliefs that include intersex, trans, and androgynous deities.

When we're learning history in school, this is one of the many things our textbooks tend to leave out: that there have always been a variety of gender expressions and identities worldwide and that many have been respected, even revered and treasured. There are records of people who were not men or women from as early as 3000 BCE (Roscoe 2000).

Generally, the more contact a place and culture has had with European and Western ideas, especially in cases of forced assimilation, and Judeo-Christian religion (oftentimes part of colonization and assimilation), the more discriminated against and rejected those with other genders are. Though there are some scholars, such as those at the TransTorah organization, who say that even ancient Judaism recognized multiple genders.

In more modern history, the singular "they" pronoun had been used in English until 1745, when grammarians of that time insisted on changing to "he" as the common pronoun (Davis 2019). Excluding eunuchs, one of the earliest gender affirming surgeries was performed in 1882. In 1895, a group of self described "androgynes" formed a support club in NY. Multiple non-binary pronouns were introduced between the 1890s and the 1970s, some of which are still in use today. During the 1950s doctors were performing surgeries on intersex children, sometimes without consent or even knowledge, to erase evidence of the intersex condition. During that era, it was also illegal to "cross-dress" and we have numerous records of people arrested and convicted for "impersonating" another gender. In 1945–6, one such trial that received national attention was that of Lucy Hicks Anderson, a Black transgender woman (though I'm not sure how she would have referred to herself at the time) who, after being convicted and serving her prison sentence, was not allowed to return to her home in CA (Snorton 2017).

Learning and knowing this history can be powerful. Recognizing our connection to a lineage, to those who came before, can reduce isolation and build internal strength. Understanding the forces that impose a rigid understanding of gender, as well as learning about the ways our gender diverse kindred resisted that over time, can be freeing.

Using tradition or creating new tradition

I've had clients who've participated in naming services in a church or synagogue, in a ceremony led by an elder, or someone giving them a "name-day or birthday" party to honor their new, gender affirming name. Some Two Spirits participate in their own sweat lodge or pow wows, and other teen and adult trans women are given a quinceañera, for example. By helping clients identify and consider traditions or ceremonies that are familiar and culturally relevant, you may be able to help them create a tradition to honor their transition or a new name. Involving their spiritual practices can add powerful meaning and emotional resources to a person's transition. Some people will also enter new faith communities and belief systems or traditions after being excluded from others. I've known a number of people who left unaccepting churches to practice religions such as Ifa, Santeria, and Wicca. I've known folx who have created affirming spiritual groups that meet and honor various belief systems and practices. Sometimes, when rejected, a person may feel they have to be a-spiritual now or there's no way to be in faith community with others.

You may be able to assist clients in processing that and exploring beliefs that honor their whole selves and affirm their spiritual and physical value. I've worked with some clients whose religion and membership in a certain faith center was a strong part of their identity. When others in the group are not accepting, use spiritual scriptures or teachings to tell the person they are wrong or in sin, and maybe suggest that the person should leave the faith group if they are not willing to stay in the closet, or "de-transition," this can create enormous pressure and internal conflict that you may need to assist your client in working through. Talking about the differences between religion and spirituality can help some clients who might be in this situation.

How to assist with practical problems during transition

Some of the people you work with may need assistance with meeting basic needs as a gender non-conforming person. Your clients may be weighing up whether to apply for a job as themselves, or to be "in the closet" or "not out" at work. They may struggle with what to do about past job referees who only know them with past name and pronouns, or a school diploma that has a former name and gender. I've had clients in small towns where there were few available jobs and the clients had to try and hide a transition indefinitely at work in order to stay employed. Some clients may be struggling with whether they can emotionally cope with going to work, where they might be mis-gendered regularly by supervisors, co-workers, and customers. Other clients who are "out" might notice they are skipped over for promotions while cisgender co-workers receive them.

Some research has shown that therapists can assist clients in expanding on coping strategies to deal with transphobia in the workplace such as developing perseverance, confidence, and self affirmation, building skills to manage strong emotions in the moment, connecting with peers for support, planning ahead for situations where stigma might be encountered, utilizing spiritual practices and supports, and ignoring and disengaging emotionally at work (Mizock & Mueser 2014).

Clinicians can also help clients weigh the pros and cons of coming out at work and in coming up with a plan for coming out, if that is the client's wish. Resources and guides on assisting employees in transition can be provided to HR departments and managers, and recommendations for workplace trainings can be provided.

One in five transgender people will face housing instability, or even homelessness (Flentje *et al.* 2016). This is because of family rejection, running away from or aging out of foster care, and employment and housing discrimination. You may need to help clients come up with housing options or locate safer housing situations. Shelters are often not safe places for trans and gender non-conforming individuals. One study reports that 28 percent of those who had tried to access a shelter were denied admittance and 44 percent of those who had stayed at a shelter left due to safety concerns related to their identity. The same study reports that TGNC2S people who are couch surfing or living on the street are twice as likely to engage in survival sex (Kattari & Begun 2017). When working with a trans client you may need to help connect them to a trans housing network. Those that exist can usually be found online or by word of mouth in the community. Many cities or states also have Facebook groups specifically for trans folx, to post requests for housing and employment options, share recommendations for resources, and more.

Trans, gender non-conforming, and Two Spirit people are over-represented in the prison population. Structural oppression can lead to involvement in underground economies, and anti-trans bias can also lead to the arrest of trans people based on the perception that they may be involved in illegal activity (White Hughto, Reisner, & Pachankis 2015). Many trans folx are placed in housing based on their assigned sex at birth. Incarcerated TGNC2S people are at high risk for physical and sexual assault and denial of medical interventions for dysphoria, such as gender affirming hormone therapy. One US study showed that only 14 percent of incarcerated transgender people were allowed to receive hormone replacement therapy (Brown 2014). Due to lack of financial access to healthcare, as well as trauma experienced by trans people in medical settings, many trans people have used "street hormones" to achieve transition and do not have access to physician prescriptions when they are incarcerated (Clark, Hughto, & Pachankis 2017). Providers within prison settings can advocate for training in all areas of staffing, as well as changes to prison policies. All clinicians can advocate for changes in the current court and prison system, acknowledging the disparity that exists at every level. If you are working with someone who has been incarcerated, you will need to assess for trauma and likely assist the person with meeting basic needs.

Currently there is no statistic capturing the number of transgender immigrants in the United States. This is, in part, due to lack of identity questions on the US census, and in part due to fear of "outing" oneself. However, the UCLA Williams Institute says there are 267,000 LGBTQ+ immigrants in the United States and so we might estimate that 15,000–50,000 or more of those are transgender. Immigration to the United States is influenced by factors related to economics, politics, family relationships, sometimes violent oppression and threat of death. Immigrants can be in search of opportunities for employment, healthcare, and more freedom to exist as a gender non-conforming person (Morales, Corbin-Gutierrez, & Wang 2013).

When working with a trans immigrant, it's important to recognize the many challenges and experiences they have faced and are currently navigating. There is still a lack of wide scholarship in this area, but one study recommends using an ecological approach in your work with gender non-conforming immigrants (Quintero *et al.* 2015). Understanding your client involves understanding different ecological systems and how interactions within and between these systems affect them. A multi-layered perspective is necessary to recognize the mental health needs, as well as needs of basic daily living, for a transgender immigrant. You will need to be able to connect your client with legal aid resources, like the Transgender Law Center or Queer Detainee Empowerment Project. We also cannot forget the abuses that trans and gender non-conforming individuals often experience when seeking asylum, as Roxana Hernandez, age 33, of Honduras, did in 2018. When she and a caravan of about 25 other gender non-conforming people arrived in California, she was detained for two weeks by Immigration and Customs Enforcement (ICE), in a facility that others described as an "ice box" that did not provide "adequate food or medical attention." She was then transferred to a transgender unit at a federal men's prison in New Mexico that contracts with ICE. The next day she was hospitalized and died "of cardiac arrest." An independent autopsy obtained by the Transgender Law Center showed that she was dehydrated and beaten while restrained before she died (Lawler 2018). What do these experiences say about the value of a transgender life? For the humanity of an immigrant? What vicarious community trauma occurs for other trans immigrants when these things take place?

Supporting changes in sexual orientation

Depending on which study you're looking at, between 22 percent and 64 percent of trans individuals who socially or medically transition report a change in sexual orientation. You can talk about this possibility with clients so that they are not taken by complete surprise if this does happen. There's no definitive explanation of why this occurs more in trans folx than the cisgender population, but some likely possibilities have to do with being able to experience oneself as a sexual being in your affirmed gender, as well as hormonal influences for some people. Transition can increase connection with one's body, confidence, and understanding of ways that a person has previously tried to navigate sex that created the least amount of dysphoria. Some people identify as asexual prior to transition and then find that they are experiencing more romantic or sexual attraction during transition. One challenge that many people tell me comes along with this is "having to come out about one more thing." People can feel like they are burdening or confusing loved ones by having them adjust to another change. For people who are in romantic partnerships when they realize a change in sexual orientation, there may be a decision-making process about what this means for the relationship. People in monogamous relationships may decide to open those or end them. Other clients have said to me, "I have no idea how to go about dating [a particular gender], I have no experience with that," or "I've never had sex with someone with a penis and am not sure how that will be." You will want to make sure that all of your clients have access to comprehensive sexual health information from a trans inclusive source. A change in sexual orientation can be a little scary and disorienting, but it can be easier when clients know that this is a common occurrence and just another part of living a full, beautiful life.

Kayson is a 20-year-old white genderqueer person who lives at home in a rural area with parents and a 22-year-old brother who is in recovery from substance abuse. When I started working with Kayson they worked full time as an office admin staff. They were not "out" to anyone as they were very involved in a conservative Christian church and most of their friends were people they'd grown up with in the church that they believed would not be supportive. At first they came out as bisexual to a sister and the members of their Bible and Beer study group. They thought this would be a more easily accepted aspect of their identity than their gender. They did not get a supportive response and were told they were living in opposition to God's Word. I shared a resource, SoulForce, with them, so that they could read other understandings of Biblical references commonly used to condemn LGBTQ+ people. They wanted to hold a workshop on LGBTQ+ identities for the church, but were dissuaded by the Bible and Beer group. They became more depressed and quit their office job as they felt too overwhelmed to work. They got a part time job cleaning their church's daycare center. I connected them with another trans young adult who was at a similar stage of identity development and the two became friends and once in a while attended LGBTQ+ events in the closest city. They came out over time to other church friends. Most reacted negatively but a few were supportive. They eventually created a plan to come out to their parents because they wanted to be able to think about pursuing gender affirming hormone therapy. They wrote a long letter for the parents and then left home for a few days to stay with a friend while the parents absorbed the news. They were allowed back home, although their parents stated that they could not use the parents' health insurance anymore for therapy or for HRT. The parents would not use Kayson's name although they did try to stop using the wrong pronouns in Kayson's presence. Kayson began searching for a new job although their sense of self worth was low and they were nervous about whether they would need to be in the closet for a while at a new job since their documents are in their "deadname." They also had to meet with the church elders about whether they could continue their job at the church daycare and continue to attend church while "out" as genderqueer and bisexual. They considered whether they would stay at the church if it meant causing a huge rift or conflict in the membership. I gave a referral for local affirming churches and a free legal service for name change and gender marker changes so that they could start that process even while still job searching. Eventually Kayson became involved in a trans affirming church congregation. The minister there offered to baptize them using their new name and pronouns as a way of honoring their transition. Kayson invited their one transgender friend and the three friends from their former church to the service and felt it was so meaningful. They have a dream of finding ways to reach young people living in conservative religious families in rural areas to show them that they have value, are not "wrong," and can still have a spiritual faith.

SELF ASSESSMENT

1. I can list 3 books, movies, or websites with accurate historical information on gender to refer clients and families to.

   a.

   b.

   c.

2. I have an awareness of how cultural and spiritual tradition can be an active part of gender transition and identity.

   True/False

3. One way that I can work with a client on coping with anti-trans bias in the workplace is:

   ....

   ....

   ....

   ....

4. In addition to providing mental healthcare to clients who are houseless, incarcerated, or undocumented, I will take these steps:

. . . .

. . . .

. . . .

. . . .

5. Here are some things to consider talking about with a client who is experiencing changes in sexual orientation:

. . . .

. . . .

. . . .

. . . .

Scenarios

A 30-year-old trans man who is a Nigerian Muslim immigrant comes to see you to talk about some problems in his relationship with his girlfriend and feelings of sadness and isolation. What are some things to consider when working with this client? What are some things you might say or ask about in the first session? What resources might you explore to share with this client?

. . . .

. . . .

. . . .

. . . .

. . . .

. . . .

A 25-year-old Mi'kmaq Two Spirit person recently began to talk more openly about how he experiences his gender. He is married to a cisgender Shawnee woman with two small children. They come to your office for housing assistance and because the spouse is struggling to understand and accept what changes might come about, as well as knowing how to talk with their children about it. What are some things to consider when working with this client? What are some things you might say or ask in the first session? What resources might you explore to share with this client?

. . . .

. . . .

. . . .

. . . .

. . . .

. . . .

CHAPTER 4

Family Work with Transgender People

One topic I'm frequently asked about by providers is how to support family members of trans and gender non-conforming people. Providers often say, "my client/patient is doing fine, but the family is struggling." People wonder how to know when to be patient and allow the family to be in a process and when a family member may need to challenged more to move into embracing change or to be confronted with the very real statistics on suicide risk and substance abuse in those who do not have supportive family. Sometimes healers can make assumptions about which families will or won't be supportive based on religion, geographic region, race and ethnicity, academic privilege, and so on, so it's important to check our biases when meeting a family. Clinicians can sometimes have a difficult time recognizing when a partner may be expressing emotion versus engaging in verbal abuse. The reality is that sometimes a trans person may need to take a break from, or completely end, a relationship that becomes toxic and harmful in connection to their gender identity. Healers can support clients in deciding if, when, and how that should happen, if needed, and in processing the painful emotions that can come with that event.

Support for partners and children during transition

When I'm working with a person who is talking about socially or medically transitioning, I remind them that any partner or family member will also be going through a transition, regardless of how supportive the person might be. Some writers have called this "co-transitioning" (Theron & Collier 2013). I also remind them that, while they may have known certain truths about themselves for some time, a partner or family member may just be hearing it or processing it for the first time.

Partners of a person who is transitioning may have to re-evaluate their own identities, such as what their identity or expression means in relation to a trans partner's. This may even be true for relationships where two or more partners are not cisgender. A partner who is co-transitioning may need to evaluate their level of attraction to a body that has changed in any number of ways and whether sexual desire is there. Partners may notice many small changes involved in attraction, such as that the person has a new smell. At the same time, a person at some point in transition may come to a new understanding of their own sexual orientation, potentially no longer being attracted to their current partner(s). The ways that partners have sex and relate to one another during sex may need to change.

Partners who are supportive might notice that the person transitioning is very focused on those steps and aspects of change. A partner trying to actively support might need encouragement to pay attention to their own needs too. They can sometimes feel disloyal in talking about any challenging emotions or aspects of the transition to other people. Oftentimes, they feel that they are unwanted in LGBTQ+ or trans inclusive spaces, but that there are no other spaces for them (Platt & Bolland 2018). Clients of non-binary partners may have difficulty relating to support spaces that tend to be solely partners of binary trans people. They may be concerned about their gender non-conforming partner's safety and feel worried or anxious. They might feel angry at seeing the partner mistreated, judged, or attacked. Sometimes, at certain points in transition, their partner may not feel comfortable being in settings or situations that they did before. A partner might then struggle with whether to stay at home more with the partner or continue to go out and do things alone or with others.

Being perceived socially as different when together, such as a couple previously viewed as lesbians now being viewed as a straight couple, may come both with privilege as well as some sense of losing the strong support of LGBTQ+ communities. Some partners who had a strong queer identity may resent feeling like that identity is lost or rendered invisible. This can be heightened if a trans partner is not "out" or openly trans and another partner feels "closeted" by this. Partners who were perceived as a straight couple may resent being viewed as gay and may experience some discrimination for the first time. A partner may question whether their own identity can stay the same or will need to expand or shift somehow. Other fears may be about whether the changes will result in loss of cultural community, religious community, or income, for example due to anti-trans or anti-Two Spirit bias.

One study of transmasculine people who were partnered at the time of starting transition found that half of the relationships ended (Meier *et al.* 2013). For relationships that are maintained, there can be enormous growth, expansion of internal and social understanding, and opportunities for advocacy and public education. Partners may talk about their own increased sense of freedom in gender roles and expression, as well as ways they used their experiences to engage in activism. Going through transition together can improve communication and enhance closeness and intimacy.

Providers can support partners by offering compassion from a trans affirming view, validating and normalizing emotions, connecting partners to online and in-person support with other partners in transition, and sharing resources such as books for partners, podcasts, and social media accounts or groups. It's important that any resource you share is one that you've personally read or viewed and know is trans affirming, or has been reviewed and endorsed by trans people. I've had clients come across online forums for partners that were places unsupportive spouses or partners were venting rage, hatred, and encouraging lawsuits and custody battles. Please review resources so you can direct partners to information that is current and not harmful to trans folx. Part of the work can involve increasing tolerance of uncertainty, managing anxiety, and staying in the present as much as possible.

Parenting as a trans person

My clients and community members with children are often worried about how their kids might be affected by their transition. In some cases, they are worried about a co-parent trying to limit their involvement or shared custody with their child due to anti-trans bias and, in fact, I've had a couple of clients who were in custody battles because of this. There's also fear that others will view the trans parent as unfit, or negatively influencing their child, resulting in Child Protective Services reports, which has also happened to some people due to anti-trans discrimination. There's been very little research on the experiences of children with trans and gender non-conforming parents but what we do know suggests that children can often understand a gender spectrum easily, can be a source of support and encouragement for a transitioning parent, and that open communication with children about transition can create a strong parent–child bond (Hines 2006). One series of interviews with transgender parents showed an increased level of conflict with a transitioning parent in older children versus younger children. There was also more conflict when the co-parent was not supportive of the transition (White & Ettner 2007).

In working with the family, or a trans person who is speaking about family issues, I tend to take the view that every family is going to experience many stressors over time. The gender transition of a parent may be just one stressor the family lives through. I ask families about what other stressful events they've experienced together. I ask what strengths and supports helped them during that time and assist them in identifying communal/relational supports, economic, spiritual, and personal/internal supports.

These may be needed to cope with the transition of a parent in the family. An intersectional framework also recognizes that some families will experience multiple stressors at the same time as a transition, or because of it, due to holding multiple marginalized identities. Some families will not have the finances to fund gender transition. Stigma might prevent other families from accessing previously utilized resources. Transition comes with more safety risks for some families than others.

Sometimes families are struggling with the question: "Am I losing my loved one? Are they going away?" Encouraging families to continue shared meaningful activities like meals, spiritual practices, playing games, or other fun family time can ease the anxiety about losing the relationship and show families that they can keep a strong relationship throughout transition. For families struggling with rigid concepts of gender or religious teachings that don't allow for transgender people, here are some strategies you might use:

- provide information about the impact of colonization, slavery, and Westernization on a larger understanding of gender

- match families with families of similar identities and socio-economic situations who are further along in transition

- share videos of supportive families of similar identities talking about their experience

- introduce families to affirming religious teachings

- have the most supportive family member talk alone with the least supportive

- share research statistics on the negative mental health and social impact of a rejecting family versus an affirming family.

In a qualitative study of adult children of transgender parents, 55.6 percent reported that their trans parent had sat down and had a discussion with them about the transition. Another 22 percent reported that they'd observed gender non-conforming behaviors from the parent for some time and 22 percent said they'd always known their parent was trans. None of the adult children reported positive or negative feelings regarding their parent's disclosure—"it just was" (Veldorale-Griffin 2014). Stressors that were identified by the children were: being bullied at school; having to change their perception of their parent, including sometimes what they called their parent; and feeling caught in the middle of a trans parent and cis parent. One child in the study reported experiencing no stressors in relation to the transition. Of the adult children in this particular study, they stated that therapy was the most important thing that helped them cope with the changes. An organization such as COLAGE: People with a Gay, Lesbian, Bisexual, Transgender, or Queer Parent can also be a support network for children and youth of parents who are gender non-conforming.

Transgender parents in the study reported resilience factors in coping with the fears of family rejection during transition to be: knowledge that transition was necessary; determination; developing ability to not absorb insults or emotions of others; and, in some cases, spiritual practices. These are things we can encourage our clients and community members in deepening.

In my own practice, over the years, I've found that children of all ages are better able to accept transition or the trans identity of a parent when it is presented as a normal occurrence rather than a trauma or terrible thing, when they are able to be around families of all kinds with parents of all gender identities, read books about other kids or teens whose parent transitions, and when co-parents affirm trans identities and the parent's transition, even if the relationship is ending in separation. There are online and in-person support groups for kids of trans parents as well. Sometimes kids collaborate with parents to decide on a new "parent" name or title that's gender neutral or reflects the affirmed gender of the parent. Our broad society today tends to be patriarchal and hetero-cis-normative, which makes it crucial for families with transgender parents to have exposure and connection with families of similar make-ups and be able to learn ways that multiple genders are spiritually or culturally significant in respect to their family. It's also imperative that all families, regardless of the gender identities within them, work to unlearn patriarchy and the centering of heterosexual and cisgender ways of being, and to actively ensure they are in community with people of all genders.

Other challenges that might be faced by transgender parents relate to the fact that mainstream society is broadly focused on a binary view of gender and erases trans identities in a myriad of ways. Families with transgender parents may have to decide what to tell children's teachers and school administrators about the trans parent's identity; how to deal with "Mother's Day" and "Father's Day" events; having to be the ones leading the way with asking for trans inclusive policies at the school; having everything taught to their child at school (and most other community groups and events) in terms of "boys" and "girls," "men" and "women," and more. Constantly having to challenge these beliefs and to struggle to be recognized and seen, having to struggle to have history accurately portrayed and stories told that include the gender non-conforming and Two Spirit people who have always been here, can be emotionally exhausting and isolating.

Supporting trans and gender non-conforming people in family building

First, it should not be assumed that a trans person, no matter the age, will desire to become a parent or be genetically related to a child. Making the assumption that a trans person will regret not engaging in fertility preservation, or focusing on transition as threatening future parenting options, comes from a hetero-centric and often patriarchal viewpoint that prioritizes reproduction and nuclear family over any other way of life. It assumes that someone's life cannot be as meaningful without being a parent.

For trans folx who *do* want to parent, there are some things to consider. According to an index produced by Transgender Europe, over 20 European countries require transgender people to be sterilized before changing the gender marker on various identity documents and government records (Nixon 2013). Other countries around the world also have this requirement. The right of transgender people to parent or reproduce has been challenged in many ways due to mis-information and anti-trans bias. Trans folx who have become parents have often faced harassment, including death threats. Despite the attempts to restrict freedom and access, many trans people are already parents or desire to become parents. Gender non-conforming people have used creativity and wisdom to create their families. Parenthood is widely viewed in highly gendered terms and roles so trans folx navigate their own identities amidst the gendered world of parenting.

Reproduction

Prior to medical transition, folx can undergo fertility preservation. Some people have also been on gender affirming hormone therapy and choose to stop it in order to do fertility preservation, fertility treatments, or conceive. Most physicians will recommend being off hormone therapy for 2–6 months before attempting conception or donation of genetic material (dickey *et al.* 2016). Results differ from person to person, just as fertility differs in cisgender people. The preservation process can exacerbate dysphoria, even when the person really wants the outcome. Interacting with fertility clinics for the process can expose the person to even more gendered spaces than typical medical centers, and fertility clinics are often not trans affirming. In your work, you should be knowledgeable about various fertility procedures and able to explain them, options for reproduction for your client, and which clinics in the area may have the most knowledge in working with transgender patients. Your client may need support in managing dysphoria and microaggressions throughout the experience.

The other thing to be aware of is that fertility preservation and fertility treatments are extremely expensive. Few insurance plans cover them, so they may be financially inaccessible to your client. For example, cryopreservation of sperm for up to five years can cost $2000–$4000, while egg retrieval and cryopreservation of eggs or embryos can cost $5000–$20,000 per ovulation cycle (Polly & Polly 2014). For those with insurance coverage, the medical provider may need to be aware of which billing codes to use for a trans patient to ensure coverage.

It's important to know (and for people you work with to know) that being on HRT is not birth control and that pregnancies can occur while on HRT. Conception while on hormone therapy can lead to increased risk of birth defects, though some people who have become pregnant on HRT have delivered babies with no birth defects (dickey *et al.* 2016).

Your clients may attempt to start families through having sex, depending on the body parts each partner has, through at home insemination with a known donor or sperm from a bank, through intrauterine insemination (IUI) or in vitro fertilization (IVF) at a clinic. They may use donor eggs or embryos or surrogacy (traditional or using a gestational carrier).

I'll share my own personal journey here, as a way to illustrate just some of the things trans people may come across during this process. My partner and I decided to pursue having a child, using my eggs and uterus. We first asked a friend to be our known sperm donor, which would have meant drawing up a legal contract and setting up monthly donation times/place. Our friend, who was much younger than us, let us know that he did not feel ready emotionally and mentally for such a process. We understood what a huge thing we were asking of someone and respected a "no"…and we also felt sad. We talked about asking other friends but decided we didn't want to risk having other conversations that might be awkward and disappointing in the small community we were part of. So we turned to sperm banks. We started searching nationwide for donors of color. We quickly learned that while most banks had hundreds or even thousands of donors, they would have anywhere from 0–20 total donors of color at a time. Once we found a donor we both liked, we realized we'd be paying $1000 per vial, which for us meant "per try." The state where we lived did not offer fertility coverage. When we met with a financial counselor at a local fertility clinic, we were given a quote and knew we needed to take out a large personal loan to be able to have several tries at insemination in clinic.

It's important to know that many clinics won't allow people to use "known donors" so, if you want to do that, you'll need to be creative in how you present and introduce your donor at a clinic to get around this. If you're like us, using sperm or eggs from a bank, you have to attend a mandatory "counseling session." We were told we had to do that with the clinic's therapist on staff. Now I know that I could have requested to do it in the community instead with an affirming provider, but I wasn't told that was an option at the time. Our "LGBTQ+ friendly" clinic did not have space on the intake forms for us to identify as other than male or female. We wrote in our gender identities and pronouns (they/them), but these were never used. When we arrived for our mandatory counseling sessions, we found we were assigned to do it with a cisgender lesbian couple. The counselor showed a video about "mothers" and "lesbian parenting." She made each couple answer questions such as "Have you thought about what parenting names you will have? Some couples use Mom and Mama," and "Have you decided who will be the 'male figure' in your child's life? Research has shown this is very important." My partner pretty much shut down and didn't speak during the session, while I got angrier and angrier and was snapping answers like "Yes, we have. Our parent names reflect our heritage and are not based on mothering," "Our child will know people of *all* genders," "What research are you referring to?" We were given a list of book resources explaining to children about having two mothers. Whenever I spoke, the counselor furiously wrote on a notepad. I thought we were going to be denied receiving sperm from the bank based on her "evaluation." The whole appointment was upsetting and infuriating. The clinic clearly never paid any attention to what we wrote on our forms and were using some really messed up stereotypes and cis-hetero-normative ideas. After we recovered, I emailed the clinic asking that they receive training on being trans affirming and gave recommendations for who could do those trainings.

One month we were so fed up with the process that we met a midwife online in a trans pregnancy group who had never done an at home insemination but was willing to try. We drove an hour into a rural area with a tank of sperm in the car to meet a total stranger who'd put on a headlamp, google instructions, and prop my legs up on hers. It took a while and hurt like hell. It wasn't successful, so we went back to the clinic next round. My partner and I then learned that, in order for the one of us who was not the gestational carrier to be listed on the birth certificate, we needed to be legally married for at least six months prior to a birth. This was not a requirement for cis-het couples, but we complied. We also knew that likely we would still have to pay for a second parent adoption for one of us to legally adopt our own child so that our parenting rights could not be questioned. After exhausting our loan, we ended up moving to another state that offers some fertility treatment coverage in their insurance plans. Unlike some states, there is no exclusion for "same gender" or "same sex" people, fortunately. We have been able to continue trying once in a while. I've had to take medications that have changed my body in ways that increase dysphoria for me. We're now at a third clinic. During our first appointment, our second clinic asked why I was the one trying to carry since my partner was younger. Both the doctor and nurse asked us this (showing no awareness of how gender identity or dysphoria might differ from person to person or play a role in these decisions). The doctor asked how long we'd been "trying." This is a standard question you're asked all the time at these clinics, which means "How long have you been regularly having sex without conceiving?" This doesn't apply to partnerships where there are some key body parts or ingredients missing for conception. I asked the doctor if he was asking how many procedures we'd done, which was on the notes in front of him or asking something else.

None of the clinics we've been to have been trans affirming in the slightest. They're fine with cis gay and lesbian partnerships. During our journey, I had a Black transmasculine client attempt to do IVF at another local clinic and be turned away, hearing "we've never worked with somebody like you before." Another couple I saw for their required "third party reproduction" letter also had frustrating experiences at a supposedly "LGBTQ friendly" facility.

While the cisgender woman was being examined, she was asked "How long have you been trying?" by the nurse. This was after listing on the paperwork and in conversation with the doctor that her partner was a trans man. After ignoring the question once, the nurse asked again, so she responded "My husband is trans. We have a lot of sex, but we don't have sperm." The nurse responded by patting her arm and saying "good for you." This was not an out of the norm medical experience, but when people have to seek medical assistance for reproduction, challenging emotions can be present and patients can feel very vulnerable, which makes these types of microaggressions even more harmful. Grants that exist to help cover the great expense of reproduction generally are not open to, or favoring of, LGBTQ+ people, especially trans folx. Along our parenting journey, we haven't talked about it a ton with our queer and trans friends, who would usually be our support. We have talked it about it with friends we know have been on a similar quest, but it's felt hard.

During this time, I've also had a queer cisgender friend be a surrogate for a gay cisgender man. I've had friends who are a gay cis man and gay gender non-conforming person enter a program called Men Having Babies that matches surrogates and provides some financial assistance, as surrogacy can be very costly. I've also had friends use "known donor" matching websites to find donors they can meet and get free sperm for at home inseminations, such as Co-Parent, Pride Angel, and Known Donor Registry. For people who have a strong desire for a genetic connection, such as people of color who might want to continue an ancestral line, having a relative donate genetic material might be an option (dickey *et al.* 2016). Sometimes people will want a genetic connection to a child and not be able to have one and there may be a grief process involved. In terms of parenting, transmasculine, non-binary, and transfeminine people may be able to chestfeed or breastfeed biological or adoptive children. La Leche League has online information on supporting this process and you may seek information from trans affirming lactation consultants or birth workers. It's exciting that some trans folx without a uterus may have a uterine transplant option in the future. There has been a successful uterine transplant with a live birth (Brännström *et al.* 2015).

There are also ways for people who want to find someone to co-parent with to connect on known donor sites. I've known of people who chose to have sex with someone who had the body parts needed to conceive in order to have a way to reproduce that didn't cost money. I've known of people who chose to co-parent with three people or as a group of people.

Fostering and adoption

While federal law does not prohibit transgender and gender non-conforming people from adopting or becoming foster parents, some states have attempted to limit these rights and it can be difficult to find an agency that accepts and embraces trans applicants. Currently, 10 states have laws allowing child welfare and adoption agencies to discriminate against LGBTQ+ applicants based on religious exemption (Movement Advancement 2018). Notice that this disproportionally hurts youth of color, especially Black youth, who are over-represented in the foster care system, by limiting the availability of foster homes and adoptive families, as well as individuals of color, who parent at higher rates than white LGBTQ+ individuals (Battle & Ashley 2008). Some agencies, however, do recruit LGBTQ+ applicants as foster parents. Some trans individuals may have to decide whether to disclose their gender identity during the application process. Attorneys usually advise to do so early in the process, as it is likely to be discovered during the background investigation process (dickey *et al.* 2016). I've known of a number of trans individuals who fostered and then adopted the children of a relative who was unable to care for the children. I've had friends do an open adoption (which cost $50,000) and other friends do a less expensive adoption, but as Black gender non-conforming people they waited for 3–4 years on a list before being chosen. Some people will co-parent a partner's existing children. I encourage these folks to seek legal advice on protection of their parenting rights, as I have known a number of LGBTQ+ people, especially trans people, who had a court rule against their parenting rights after separation from the other parent.

Family work

During trainings, one of the most common things I'm asked about is how to support families through a family member's transition. To understand why family members may respond to a child or loved one's transition with shock, fear, anger, loss, or sadness, we have to recognize the degree to which, in mainstream society, gender is used as a primary source of making sense of human behavior and the world. Oftentimes a fear of "losing" the person or belief that they are "turning into someone different" is an initial reaction. In the past, therapists were encouraged to walk families of trans individuals through the "Stages of Grief." However, more recent research suggests that reconciling the presence and the absence, the sameness and the difference, of their child is a unique challenge for parents (Norwood 2013), and that an ambiguous (confusing, without clear rituals) loss perspective can be particularly helpful. Helping families hold complexity and consider ways to make meaning and ritual during change is one way therapists can assist in the process. This quote represents an idea that I talk with family members about: "When an event of loss cannot be changed, the only window for change lies in shifting one's perception of that event" (Boss 2004).

For families struggling with the "presence" question: "Is my child still here?," presence activities can counterbalance the fear: shared meals, continuing shared spiritual activities, or family outings. Encouraging families to maintain their relationship and maintain quality family time is important during transition. Family members may also need to be encouraged to take breaks from talking about gender identity and to manage anxiety by accessing friends or professional support, spiritual practice, physical exercise, and more, rather than trying to relieve that anxiety through constantly asking questions of their loved one.

For families struggling with rigid gender notions, education related to when/where binary gender notions came from can help. Matching families for conversation with families of similar culture, race, religion, and socioeconomic status (SES) who are further along in a family member's transition can help. For families struggling with their religion's teachings about gender identity, sharing trans affirming resources based on that religion or having them speak with a trans affirming religious leader can be helpful. Sometimes it can help to have a supportive family member talk to another family member who is struggling to accept or feeling resistant. You can also provide families with the research showing the vast difference in mental health and overall functioning of those with family support versus those without. Sometimes a straightforward conversation about the real risks of suicide or substance abuse can help families recognize that they do want to be supportive and affirming. You can assist families in looking at other times in family history that they have been resilient and come together after a difficult time. Family members can be reminded of their own strength and ability to get through hard times.

CASE EXAMPLE

I worked with one white, blended family adjusting to one parent's transition. The kids ranged from elementary through high school ages and we had some family sessions so that some of their questions could be answered about what transition meant and might be like. Things that were brought up in these sessions by the kids were: "How do we tell our friends?" "My brother hasn't told the neighborhood kids yet and it's awkward when they come over," "Our other parent and step-parent don't really understand this so how do we handle inappropriate comments from them?" and "I get mad when people at school say bad things about trans people." Through conversation and role-plays of various scenarios, the family members all felt more confident in answering questions, as well as negative comments from others.

CASE EXAMPLE

I worked with another multi-cultural family, Black and Latinx, where one parent was gender non-conforming and the teen was starting to transition. Things that came up in these sessions were:

- "We don't want people to think we influenced her to be trans because we're LGBTQ+."

- "How do we tell if her mood swings are from hormone therapy or just part of being a teenager?"

- "We want to go to the family support group in town but then we're the only family of color there so we still feel like we have different issues than the other families."

The parents responded well to education on gender affirming hormone therapy, parenting coaching, and were able to meet other families of color who were affirming of their trans youth as well.

Partner work

Another aspect of therapy in working with TGNC2S adults is relationship therapy or work with partners of a person who is transitioning. During consultation, I'm often asked how to help recognize whether a partner's feelings are "justified" or "abusive." Trans individuals can have a hard time distinguishing this as well. We talk about how emotions are always okay, but each of us is responsible for how we express and communicate them. Someone can share their feelings assertively and effectively or they can choose abusive behaviors. Whether you are working with a partner or a person transitioning, you may need to be able to assist your client in assessing this. Some ways to recognize abusive dynamics are if one person is attempting to control the gender expression of the other; when one person threatens to "out" the other in situations where the person is not ready or safe to be "out"; when one person threatens to disclose STI/HIV status of the partner to others; when one person threatens to have trans community shun the other person; when one person actively refuses to use correct name and pronouns; when one person mocks the other for being cisgender; when a cis partner threatens to cut off a trans partner from access to the children, and so on.

There are many ways relationships can choose to adapt to new information about one partner's gender identity. Some decide to try to continue and strengthen their relationship, some decide to amicably go separate ways, perhaps maintaining a friendship, and others decide to stay together in an open or non-monogamous relationship.

CASE EXAMPLE

Cindra is a Native (Tuscarora) trans woman who is married to a cisgender white woman, Lisa. Cindra and Lisa had been married for 10 years before Cindra came out to Lisa. They lived in a conservative community and Lisa had a home daycare. Cindra worked as a mechanic and wasn't sure if transitioning would mean being fired from work. She was worried Lisa would leave her. Lisa had some feelings of sadness at first, and fear, but, after about a year, she began to be able to be fully supportive and said that she knew she wanted to stay married to Cindra. They talked about ways their sexual relationship might change, but both felt okay with the changes. Cindra's workplace was a mixture of supportive and unsupportive co-workers and she kept her job. Lisa lost a couple of children from her home daycare because their parents had anti-trans bias, but she was able to fill their spots fairly quickly. Cindra's family was supportive and this helped Lisa too. Lisa had one good friend whom she confided her feelings in regularly throughout the process. Although the friend didn't know much about the gender spectrum before, she was a good listener and supportive of both Lisa and Cindra. Two years into transition, the couple says they are stronger than before.

CASE EXAMPLE

Dane is a white trans man who is with Tam, a mixed race person who was adopted and did not have definitive information about their ethnicity. Dane and Tam got together when Dane was identifying as genderqueer about two years ago. Tam identified as non-binary. Dane came to understand themselves as male and started to medically transition with hormone therapy. Tam was supportive from the start. As the next year went on, Tam began to notice that Dane seemed distant and secretive. It came to Tam's attention that Dane was having an affair with a white cisgender female co-worker. This presented a crisis in the relationship and Tam requested couples therapy. Dane began to express uncertainty about his sexual orientation and began to share negative feelings about Tam's non-binary identity and fluid gender expression. It became evident that Dane was wanting to experience his sexuality in various encounters with his affirmed gender and body that he was becoming more confident in. He also seemed to have some internalized negative messaging related to femininity and was reacting to Tam negatively when Tam had a more femme expression or was perceived as female in public. Tam had been the identified support person to help with surgery recovery after Dane's hysterectomy and Dane still wanted this to happen. Tam had become clear that the relationship needed to end so that Tam could work on personal healing and eventually be in a relationship where Tam's gender identity was validated and celebrated as well. However, Tam did still care for Dane after surgery and sought emotional support from friends. The two then ended contact so that they could each grieve the break up and work on healing individually.

Parenting work

Sometimes a trans client will have children they are co-parenting and their transition will bring about conflict with the other parent. Your client may need legal resources to seek advice and consultation on their parental rights. They may have challenging choices to make if the other parent is withholding access to their child or undermining their relationship and teaching transphobic things to their children.

CASE EXAMPLE

Jessica is a white woman of trans experience who came out first to her cisgender, white wife. Her wife reacted with rage and disgust and began divorce proceedings. Jessica was taken by surprise, as her wife expressed "liberal" viewpoints and politics. Jessica and her wife were able to use mediation to come up with a separation agreement. Jessica's wife sought out her own therapy, but refused to see a trans affirming therapist. She would also insult me with transphobic comments to Jessica on the days of our sessions, which was upsetting to Jessica. Jessica got a small apartment and was paying child support, but was very financially strained although she had a good income. She was able to come out at work and be somewhat supported there. Her ex-wife began to express concerns about the children who were in elementary school finding out and stated that they would not be able to handle this. Jessica was worried that she would lose access to the children if she came out to them or presented as female when they were staying with her. I provided referrals for legal consultation and trans affirming children's therapists. For two years, Jessica dropped the children off at school, then changed into her clothing and wig in the bathroom of our therapy office or the bathroom of her workplace. On the days she had the children in the evening after school, she also changed back out of her clothing and wig before leaving work to pick them up.

After two years of this, Jessica's ex-wife agreed that she could talk with the children about her gender and that she could start to present as female when she had them. She still was not comfortable with the school or other school parents knowing and stated that she did not want the children losing friendships or experiencing discrimination over this. So, at this point, Jessica still had to change in and out of clothing for school pick ups and drop offs, but could be herself all the time at home. We had planned ahead for some children's books about parents transitioning that she read to her children and answered questions they had. The youngest child took things easily in stride, even quickly starting to tell her she was "pretty" and that her blue dress looked really nice on her. The older child had more difficulty adjusting. She expressed that she still wanted a "Dad" and did not want "two Moms." She seemed visibly uncomfortable at times seeing my client in feminine attire and make-up. My client validated these feelings and said that she could still call her Dad when they were at home together, and that out in public she could say "Jessica," if that was more comfortable than "Mom." This was their arrangement for some time. She was very patient with her child and we discussed the balance between validating emotions and not pushing her child too quickly, while at the same time, not allowing emotions or challenges to send her back into the closet. After a few more months, she was able to successfully advocate with her co-parent to come out to the school and they discussed how they would handle any questions or negativity from other parents. At this point her ex-wife had become more accepting of her transition and they were moving towards establishing a friendship. The older child's anxiety eased as she saw her mother become more accepting and validating of her trans parent's identity and expression.

CASE EXAMPLE

My Iranian American trans woman client had been feeling like the other mother of her child, a white cisgender bisexual woman, was supportive of her transition as they began talking about it. However, when my client's child saw a dress at the house and my client explained that it was her dress and tried to explain her gender, the co-parent reacted very strongly and began court proceedings to gain full custody. My client was shocked, hurt, and afraid. I was able to provide legal resources and they attempted mediation, but it did not go well and led to court proceedings. My client's anxiety increased and, along with that, dissociation occurred at times. It was very difficult for her to maintain employment while feeling so distraught. We worked on grounding and regulating the nervous system. I validated the discrimination and anti-trans bias that was occurring. We worked on identifying her internal and external strength and resources and ways to draw on those. She had developed some supportive friendships and also began writing music with a friend, which was an outlet for her emotions.

SELF ASSESSMENT

1. Here are two ways I can support partners and children of people who are in transition:

   . . . .

   . . . .

   . . . .

   . . . .

   . . . .

2. Here are two things I need to be knowledgeable about so that I can support trans folx in building families:

   . . . .

   . . . .

   . . . .

   . . . .

   . . . .

3. Here is one way trans parents or potential parents can be discriminated against:

....

....

....

....

....

4. Here are two resources I could share with prospective or current transgender parents:

....

....

....

....

....

Scenarios

Javier is a single, pansexual Puerto Rican trans man renting an apartment, who is interested in becoming a foster parent and potentially adopting a child. He is worried about whether an agency will view him negatively due to any of his identities or status as a renter. He is also wondering what type of support he could have as an LGBTQ+ foster parent. Discuss how you would support Javier, what resources you would assist with, etc.

....

....

....

....

....
....
....
....
....

Chrystal is a Black queer woman of trans experience who is partnered with a white genderfluid person named Casey. Casey has a four-year-old child from a previous marriage who primarily lives with Casey. For two years now, Chrystal has been acting as a co-parent with Casey. Discuss how you would support both Chrystal and Casey, as well as the child, as they are becoming family.

....
....
....
....
....
....
....
....
....

The Ukrainian immigrant parent of your client (a genderqueer youth who is planning to start gender affirming hormone therapy: estradiol and spironolactone in this case) is demanding that the youth go through fertility preservation prior to starting HRT as the parent insists that the youth could not know whether they want biological children in 15 years, and that the parent would not be doing their duty if they did not make the young person preserve fertility. Discuss how you would handle this:

. . . .

. . . .

. . . .

. . . .

. . . .

. . . .

. . . .

. . . .

. . . .

CHAPTER 5

Medical Transition Options and Considerations

Hopefully, at this point, you're aware that there are many genders, not just two. That awareness needs to lead to a shift that enables you to avoid assuming you know a person's gender when you see them or meet them. This message is for all of us. I have been mis-gendered almost as often by my binary trans clients as I have cisgender strangers. This knowledge of multiple genders will better allow you to understand your client's identity, whether demi-boy, transfeminine, winkte, genderqueer, or boi/gui, for example, and how that may differ from their gender expression. Hopefully, at this point, we also know that people may socially transition in any number of ways or medically transition in any number of ways. Some people may not medically transition at all due to lack of access to financial resources, safety issues that may increase with medical transition, not feeling that available medical procedures can address their particular dysphoria, or for cultural or spiritual reasons.

Gender affirming hormone therapy

If a client expresses to you a desire to access gender affirming hormone therapy, please know that if utilizing a provider who uses the Informed Consent model (an alternative approach to the WPATH (World Professional Association on Transgender Health) Standards of Care), they do not need a referral letter from you. WPATH standards also do not require a letter for HRT, but some providers who do not use Informed Consent do ask for one.

Also know that you may work with some folx who share with you that they are "DIY-ing" their hormones, ordering the medications online, taking extra medications from friends, or buying from "the street" and managing their own dosages through research in social media forums, word of mouth, and medical papers. It's important not to judge people who are doing this or attempt to emphasize consequences, but to understand that this is the result of structures of classism and racism, as well as transphobia. If someone doesn't have access to trans affirming medical care due to lack of health insurance and financial means, living in an area without trans competent providers, or at home with family who will not allow them to begin hormone therapy, this may be a person's only way to manage dysphoria. In these cases, you can work to find medical resources that are accessible to your client. You can also work to review risks and benefits with your client to make sure they are as informed as possible. You can make sure your client understands the risks of injecting themselves and dangers of sharing needles, as well as being aware of any needle exchange programs in your area. You'll want to understand your client's view of the mental health benefits of hormone therapy versus any physical risks they may choose to take on. Taking a harm reduction approach is beneficial with any gender affirming behavior your client is engaging in.

The Informed Consent model is centered in the patient's bodily autonomy or sovereignty, harm reduction, and self determination and agency in decision-making. It challenges the notion of provider as expert and the one who determines "readiness" for medical transition. A provider using Informed Consent will give information on the risks and benefits of a medical intervention and discuss possible alternatives. Whenever I talk about Informed Consent, I'm always asked "What about someone with active psychosis or Down's Syndrome? It's not ethical to just give them a medical intervention because they asked when they're not able to comprehend the effects or follow medical directions." Informed Consent means that you are not assuming a patient with any sort of psychosis, cognitive delay, or neurodiversity cannot adequately give consent. You are working with that person to ensure you're presenting information in a format that's most accessible to that person, working to ensure that they have whatever supports in place are possible to assist them with administering medications or caring for surgical wounds. This preparation work may take extra time and creativity. It won't happen in one meeting. But it is unethical to simply state that someone can't give consent and to deny them gender affirming care. At the same time, it is the case that not everyone has access to a perfect recovery scenario either. We do our best to connect a client with every resource available, but we also accept that a less than ideal plan is not a reason to deny care as ideal circumstances are not equally available to all people.

In regards to Informed Consent, another thing I've heard a few times is "It's not fair to expect medical professionals to go against their medical judgment. Surgeons (or physicians) shouldn't have to provide a service they don't feel is necessary, or will have good medical outcomes." Here, I will just say that I'm a strong advocate of body autonomy. I believe that a person should be able to access a gender affirming medical service if they want it. I don't believe that medical professionals should be the ones deciding what each human values most—their medical health, the visible appearance of results, the functionality of results, or their spiritual and mental wellbeing. While it's probably realistic to say that most of us don't want to have a complication from a procedure or a negative outcome, I've heard many gender non-conforming people say that they are aware of risks and feel that, if the absolute worst thing happened, they would still be glad they were able to have a gender affirming procedure.

To put this in perspective, Turtle Island (the United States), has an extremely high mortality rate for childbirth. Our medical institutions don't have a great track record for managing complications during and after birth. Yet, I haven't heard anyone arguing that we should be limiting someone's right to give birth or access to obstetrical care because it's a risky and dangerous act to give birth and be a patient in our hospital birthing wards. No organization has instituted requirements such as needing 6–12 months of therapy, or two recommendation letters from a social worker and a psychologist, before being allowed to give birth. The same people who have great concerns about trans folx with a range of other conditions being able and "ready" to access medical services are silent about people with uteruses being able to embark on the potentially life-threatening journey of childbirth. I don't hear the same concerns voiced. I hope we can see that this difference is due to mainstream society's gender lens and deeply rooted beliefs and biases about gender identities, gender roles, and, frankly, internalized anti-trans bias even amongst some trans advocates who take issue with Informed Consent models.

Most affirming centers and practices for transgender healthcare today are using Informed Consent, but it's important to know about WPATH Standards of Care (SOC) as well. WPATH is an international organization that was originally formed in 1979 under the name Harry Benjamin International Gender Dysphoria Association, after Dr. Harry Benjamin, a German endocrinologist and sexologist who assisted patients of all ages in medical transition in the 1950s and 1960s. That association created the first international clinical Standards of Care for people seeking social, hormonal, or surgical transition services, using Dr. Benjamin's case studies as a guide. The SOC are periodically revised and updated, with the most recent, Version 7, being updated in 2011. Another version is currently being drafted. The SOC includes guidelines on things such as treatment of children, adolescents, and adults, mental health, HRT (or gender affirming hormone therapy), reproductive health, voice and communication therapy, gender affirming surgeries, preventative and primary care, applicability of the WPATH SOC to people living in institutional environments, and applicability of the WPATH SOC to people with intersex conditions or differences of sex development. The SOC sets forth the requirements for different procedures.

Just a few of the critiques that many have had of WPATH as an organization, over time, are that historically there has been much less trans representation on committees creating the standards, especially trans people of color. Many have felt that the guidelines were unnecessarily restrictive, placing hardships on trans folx, in particular trans women and children or adolescents. There has been language considered offensive, such as referencing intersex conditions, which could be viewed as simply part of a range of chromosomal, hormonal, and genital combinations, instead as "Disorders of Sex Development." There have been critiques of the "certification" program WPATH developed, which is financially inaccessible to many, especially to some trans identified providers. Others have criticized the organization for holding its international conferences in countries outside of the United States and Europe, having a majority of attendees fly in from Western countries, and then not adequately honoring the land the conference is held on, or making it accessible for local citizens to attend and present as experts on their lived experiences in that location.

However, given that many insurance companies and medical providers use WPATH SOC for approving care, it is important for you to know the current requirements so you can assist clients in accessing affirming services. It's also important because I've encountered some providers who are using requirements from SOC Version 6 or even 5 and I've had to inform them of the update and share the newest version in order to advocate for a client. I've also seen insurance companies creating their own criteria based on outdated SOC and insisting they are within their rights to do so. If this is happening with a company in your state, you may need to collaborate with other providers and advocacy groups to request meetings with them to ask that they use current SOC. If you encounter a surgeon who is using outdated requirements, you may also need to meet with them, as well as assist a client in finding a surgeon who does.

I'm going to share a couple of examples of surgery referral letters. These are not the only ways letters can be written by any means, but a general guide for those who are new to the practice or wondering about other ways. My preference is to keep a letter short, to the point, and addressing the criteria. I ask clients if they want to see the letter and give feedback before it's sent. Sometimes clients want to take the letter with them. Some clients want to see it first and others don't. (Reminder that all names and identifying information are changed throughout this book.)

I've had many clients with non-binary identities seek various medical transition services. Because WPATH SOC have not previously done the best at specifying and explaining how SOC apply to non-binary people, my clients have run into surgeons refusing to treat them because their narrative is not what the surgeon is used to in working with binary trans individuals, or the required paperwork is binary gendered. After one client who was seeking chest masculinization surgery had a surgeon state "I need more documentation because I don't really understand these 'in-between type' genders," I responded with something like this:

To whom it may concern

This letter is again to recommend Tae-Young Park for chest masculinization surgery. He was in group therapy for transgender individuals with me from July 2013 to January 2014 and his anxiety is adequately managed. He was expressing his felt gender throughout our work together. There are no mental health symptoms or cognitive conditions that would be cause for delay. Tae-Young has a strong local support system.

Please refer to this informational sheet from UCSF's Center for Excellence on Transgender Health, regarding chest surgery for non-binary individuals: http://transhealth. ucsf.edu/trans?page=guidelines-gender-nonconforming.

In my practice I've had a number of non-binary trans people choose a variety of gender affirming surgeries, HRT, or other interventions to alleviate gender dysphoria and allow their bodies to more closely align with their felt gender. There is a surgeon at xxxxxxx who has done these

---

surgeries for a number of my clients if you would like to consult with her.

Sincerely,

Many of my transmasculine clients will seek a hysterectomy. Right now, the requirement is for two referral letters for this surgery. Here is an example of a second letter for this surgery.

This letter is to confirm that I am in agreement with the first letter of recommendation for hysterectomy for Tyson Smith, completed by _____. Based on my assessment and my extensive experience with transgender and gender non-conforming individuals, I confidently recommend Tyson Smith for hysterectomy surgery.

1. Tyson meets criteria for F64.1 Gender Dysphoria in Adolescents and Adults. He has masculinized his appearance through gender affirming hormone therapy and chest masculinization and this surgery is the next step in his medical transition. He was under the care of xxxxxxx for gender transition services and mental health support since 2017. 2. I met with Tyson on 3/01/2019 upon request for a second letter of support for gender affirming chest surgery. This next step in transition would decrease dysphoria further and is a recommended medical intervention for those who have been on HRT. There is no current mental health condition that would be cause for delay in receiving surgery. 3. Tyson does not exhibit psychotic symptoms or cognitive delays that would be cause for more lengthy therapy to ensure the ability to give informed consent. He is aware of the risks and benefits of surgery and meets the WPATH 2016 Standards of Care criteria. 4. Tyson has a post-surgery recovery plan and support in place. His girlfriend and an uncle will be his primary caretakers during surgery recovery. He will have time off from work to recover and is aware of post-surgical

needs. He has been saving money to assist with bills during his time away from work.

Please contact me with any concerns and see below applicable SOC (I often paste the standard into my letters).

Sincerely,

Surgery support

Often I'm able to write a letter for someone after one session. Other times it may take multiple sessions to ensure that there is informed consent and adequate planning or commitment to work in therapy while on a wait list to create a solid post-surgical plan. These would be in addition to your general psychosocial assessment or mini mental status exam. Here are some questions you might want to ask to help a client prepare for a consultation with a surgeon (they are hiring someone and a consult is like an interview) as well as to plan for the recovery period.

I make sure folx know in the beginning that their answers will not in any way keep them from getting surgery, but are for our planning purposes so they can have the best experience possible.

- What do you know about this particular surgery?

- What do you know about the risks of complications?

- When are you hoping to have the surgery and is there a certain reason that that time is best for you?

- Who knows that you're planning to have this surgery? Are they supportive? In what ways?

- What other actions to affirm your gender or relieve dysphoria have you taken in the past or want to take in the future?

- What's your living situation? How long have you been there? What's your relationship like with anyone else living there?

Do you have your own room? Do the people you live with know you'll be having this surgery?

- If employed, have you thought about what, if anything, you'll disclose about a need for time off? Do you know if your employer will give you the time off? Do you have ideas about how to pay bills while you are on leave from work? How much will you need for expenses during that time?

- What form of transportation do you use? How do you plan to get to your surgery consultation? You'll need someone to be at the hospital during the surgery and to help you get home. Do you know who that person would be?

- Do you know if you have any insurance coverage for this surgery? If not, do you know the cost? What are some ideas you have about coming up with funds?

- How do you tend to do with getting to medical appointments and taking medications?

- Have you had anesthesia before? Do you have any concerns or fears about being under anesthesia in a hospital?

- Do you have a history of any medical problems?

- Do you use any substances, including cigarettes? What do you know about any risks associated with these and surgery?

- What would you do if you thought you were experiencing a complication?

- If you needed a revision after surgery, would you return to the same surgeon, or seek a different one?

- What results are you looking for in terms of appearance and functionality?

- What are you looking forward to about having this surgery and after?

- Is there anything you're sad about in having this surgery? Afraid of?

- Who are you comfortable with helping you daily for some time after surgery with preparing food? Changing bandages or cleaning drains? Showering? Moving around?

- How do you think you'd pass the time while needing to be in bed? Reading? Watching movies? Sewing? Beading? Video games?

- Have you talked to anybody who's had this surgery?

- Will you feel more comfortable having someone go with you to your consultation? Who might that be?

Then we go into questions to help with meeting with a surgeon for consultation. Here are some examples of those:

- Do you know which surgeons you might be interested in meeting with?

- Have you talked with the finance department to find out if they are in-network or out-of-network and the fees for consultation, as well as surgery?

In a meeting:

- Ask what options of procedure types they do for this surgery.

- Ask how many they've done.

- Ask to see photos of not only their best work, but also results that required revisions.

- Ask about the rate of complications they have and what complications are most likely, as well as what they want patients to do if experiencing complication.

- Ask if they refuse surgeries based on BMI (body mass index), use of nicotine or substances.

- Ask what recovery plan and time for recovery they recommend.

- Ask how the whole team does with transgender patients and what you might expect from other staff.

- Ask if you'll need to stay overnight and if they offer a facility for recovery, especially if out of town.

- Ask when follow up appointments would be and how many.

- Ask what medications they'll likely prescribe and what to expect in terms of post-recovery pain.

- Ask whether the facility helps connect patients to any home health aide care or physical therapy afterwards.

It's great if your client can get any of these answers prior to having to pay for an expensive appointment, but, either way, these are just a start on the information a client would want in making a decision.

Before a surgery, check in with your client to make sure there haven't been last minute changes to the aftercare plan or person/people helping with recovery that they need support in planning for again.

After a surgery, your client may want to process any number of related issues: depressed mood following anesthesia, any mis-gendering or upsetting experience with hospital staff, conflicting feelings when first viewing results, disappointment in results, worry about finances, challenges with aftercare process or exercises. They also may want to share feelings of joy and relief with you and discuss how they are navigating life with the changes. Be careful to be where your client is after surgery, rather than assuming their experience.

Many times your clients may not have insurance coverage for surgery and may need help in exploring ideas about how to save money, raise money, or find a job that offers an insurance plan covering trans healthcare. Some may choose to travel out of your country to receive lower cost surgery if possible. You can assist your client in this, including researching any available scholarship or grant funds, such as Point 5cc, Jim Collins Foundation, or Trans United with Family and Friends. I've noticed that a lot of my people struggle with believing we're worth help or that we deserve to receive generosity or benefits. One thing you can do is to advocate for legislation in your state that requires coverage for trans healthcare. Another thing you can do is to advocate for your agency or organization to start a foundation that provides grant funding for surgeries and other gender affirming materials and items.

Sexual health

An area that is often overlooked by mental health and behavioral health providers is sexual health. It seems to me that many providers are uncomfortable talking about sex with clients, or believe that it's outside of the realm of what they should be addressing. If we're working to improve overall wellbeing and positive feelings and experiences, then, for many people, sexuality is part of life that we don't want to ignore. We want to assist the folx we work with in having safer sexual experiences that are consensual and without abuse or discrimination. In order to do this, we have to be able to talk freely. We can ask clients how they talk about their own sexual experiences and what names they use for their body parts. We need to be able to say words like "penetration," "receiving," "orgasm/come/cum," "ejaculate," "anal," "clit," "top," "bottom," and many more terms that our clients may use, so that we can ask questions and know what would be helpful information for our clients. We need to create a comfortable space for clients to bring up questions about their sexuality or express feelings related to sexual experiences.

Topics that are often brought up by clients:

- "I want to enjoy penetration but it's painful."

- "I'm worried that HRT will cause me to lose my libido or be unable to get hard."

- "I miss nipple sensation during sex."

- "I need to stay on my anxiety medication but it takes away my sex drive."

- "I dissociate a lot of times during sex and don't know how to stop."

- "How can I change the ways I communicate with partners about sex that is more gender affirming for me?"

- "I'm sexually interested in cis men now but don't know much about having sex with one. I want to be safe, but not really sure how."

- "I'm developing feelings for someone who I was just viewing as trade."

- "I'm afraid for my safety when meeting up with cis men for dates on dating apps."

- "Can you talk to my teen about sex because I don't know anything about how transgender people have sex?"

A lot of folx I work with want to talk about how to communicate to potential sexual partners about their wants, needs, and boundaries. Your clients may be learning what it means to get and give enthusiastic consent for any sort of physical intimacy and want to talk through examples.

As providers, we need to be able to talk about sexual pleasure and sexual health, as part of achieving overall balance in wellbeing. Because there is generally no comprehensive trans inclusive sexual health class that everyone receives growing up, many people don't know all this information or sometimes have heard misinformation that's spread around. I'm often asked in trainings "What do we do about risky sexual behaviors clients are engaging in?" As I've talked about throughout the book, I think a harm reduction approach is a respectful approach to take. Talk with your client about the most and least risky behaviors (this means you have to be informed). Try to understand the reasons your client is engaging in risky behaviors. If there are systemic factors at play, recognize which of those might be able to be addressed and which are outside of your client's (and your) control.

Part of what comes up in those questions in trainings is about clients who are engaged in sex work. In the 2015 discrimination survey by the National Center for Transgender Equality (Fitzgerald *et al.* 2015), Black and Black multiracial respondents had the highest percent of participation in the sex trade, at 39.9 percent, followed by Latinas/Latinx/Latines at 33.2 percent. White only respondents were engaged in sex trade at the lowest rate of 6.3 percent. Transfeminine respondents were twice as likely to participate than transmasculine respondents. The majority of sex workers (69.3%) reported negative experiences in the mainstream workforce, such as not being hired, being fired, or denied promotion due to gender expression or identity, and almost half had experienced homelessness. These are only a few of the forms of structural discrimination experienced by trans sex workers. Commercial sex can offer more freedom, more financial access and resources, to people who experience large degrees of social discrimination. However, many people also experience more discrimination when engaged in sex work and more traumatic experiences.

Commercial sex exists in many forms, but some forms are much more criminalized and prosecuted than others. People doing outdoor sex work are much more targeted by police, as are transfeminine people of color. Police may profile people they believe are doing this work, they might intend to target people living with HIV for prosecution, and there are reports of police destroying condoms found on sex workers, as well as using the presence of multiple condoms as grounds for arrest (Fitzgerald *et al.* 2015).

Offering support to clients engaged in sex work might mean assisting with safety planning, connecting to resources like Sex Worker's Outreach Project (SWOP), and advocating for efforts to decriminalize sex work to increase safety from assaults and reduce sexually transmitted infections (STIs).

You can find out what your clients know or don't know about various barrier methods such as internal and external condoms with water-based lube, dental dams and condoms for oral sex and rimming, latex gloves, how to use barrier methods with sex toys, and the fact that barrier methods don't always protect against STIs that can spread with close skin contact. People on testosterone (T) may experience more dryness or tear more easily during sex. People recovering from any genital surgery may also experience more tears. This makes condoms and lube even more important. After gender affirming genital surgeries, your client may have challenges with finding the right barrier method. Finger cots and parts of latex gloves can be used, and the receptive partner can use an internal condom. These (usually called female condoms) can be used internally or externally. You'll want to know where you client can easily get these items and that they can substitute plastic wrap for dams which can be hard to find and expensive. Better yet, your office can stock these items on a shelf or in the bathroom for clients to take for free. A collaborative space I used to work in (and still love) did this and it was really appreciated. A good resource to reference is Whitman-Walker Health's *Safer Sex for Trans Bodies* (n.d).

Your clients may decide to be vaccinated for some STIs such as Hep A, B, and HPV.

You also want to encourage regular screening for STIs for clients who are sexually active. Know where they can go for screening in an affirming, accessible environment.

Make sure your clients know about post-exposure prophylaxis (PEP) in the case of sexual activity where they are unsure about their exposure to HIV; it must be taken within 72 hours and taken for 28 days. It's also important to know where your clients can receive prescriptions for pre-exposure prophylaxis (PrEP) which reduces the risk of HIV. PrEP takes at least seven days of daily use to reach effectiveness with anal tissue and at least 21 days for effectiveness with front hole tissue.

People living with HIV and taking antiretrovirals (ARVs) will have their hormone levels monitored and balance of medications sought, so it's safest if folx let their HIV doctor know about unprescribed hormones they might be taking. Obviously some clients might fear repercussions from a doctor about this, and you may be able to speak with a particular HIV healthcare team first to learn their approach in that situation, so that your client can be informed. The risk of someone contracting HIV from a person consistently taking ARVs is extremely low.

In terms of birth control, people on T cannot take oral contraceptives or the "morning after" pill (and some people of various gender identities will not want to due to the levels of estrogen or progesterone they use); some intra-uterine devices (IUDs) may be options. Testosterone is not birth control and pregnancies can occur when a person is on T.

Clients who are trying to conceive should know that finasteride taken for hair loss can be harmful to fertility.

For gender non-conforming clients who want to terminate a pregnancy, you might recommend an affirming abortion doula for support.

Your client may need to continue some preventative care and screenings despite gender affirming medical services or they may have new types of screenings to adjust to. Some of these appointments can be really upsetting or hard to manage, due to dysphoria, and experiences of racism or anti-trans bias from providers. Folx may need help in thinking through upcoming appointments and how they want to advocate for themselves or who they might want to take along for support.

Some examples of self advocacy are: "Can I insert the ultrasound wand myself?," "Can you refer to my parts as xxxx or refrain from saying xxxx?," or taking in a printed card or handout explaining gender identity, pronouns, anything they want the provider to know, such as "I am a sexual assault survivor" or "Please tell me what you are going to do before touching me."

CASE EXAMPLE: GENDER AFFIRMING HORMONE THERAPY

Mariah, a Haitian trans woman, had originally obtained hormone therapy through the campus health center when she was enrolled as a university student. Due to mental health challenges and experiences of oppression on campus from other students and campus security, she had to withdraw from school and then lost her housing and access to hormones. She became very depressed. She was able to get a few hours of paid work weekly at a local LGBTQ+ center as an admin assistant, but this did not pay enough for housing and hormones. She found a queer couple who allowed her to live rent-free in their spare room. Mariah started web-cam ("camming") sex work in order to get the funds to pay for hormone therapy, doctor's appointments to monitor hormones, and low-fee therapy appointments to support mental health. Her goal was to be able to move into her own apartment or move in with one other roommate eventually.

CASE EXAMPLES: GENDER AFFIRMING SURGERY

Rodrigo, who identifies as a Latino man of trans experience, came to me for a second surgery letter required by his insurance for chest masculinization. He had spoken to several providers over the previous few weeks who were located closer to his home but was told by each that they would need to see him for a minimum of three months prior to writing the second letter for him. He was not experiencing any emotional distress other than dysphoria related to fear that a visible chest might out him when in public. Surgery would give him more peace of mind about this. He had obtained legal name change and gender marker change one year prior to meeting with me. I saw him for one session and we worked on developing other questions he had for his surgeon regarding outcomes and how to recognize complications, and details for his recovery plan, including how ways to get assistance for rent and utilities since he only had one paid week off from work and needed four weeks off. I reviewed his first letter and was able to confidently write his second letter.

Kingston is a white non-binary trans person who I'd been working with for one year. They decided that a surgery that would best alleviate their particular dysphoria would be a "breast reduction" surgery versus "masculinization." They only wanted to decrease the size so that binders would be more comfortable but did not want a more "masculine" chest. The application for surgery with the surgeon they wanted was only worded for binary trans people and they were worried they would not be approved based on this. I spoke with the surgeon to explain how this surgery was medically necessary to alleviate dysphoria and encouraged a change to the application form. The client did decide together with the surgeon to classify the surgery as "breast reduction" in order to get insurance coverage.

Sophia is an Iranian Muslim non-binary femme who decided on a hair transplant due to severely receded hairline that they felt made it impossible to appear feminine. Their family helped with the cost.

Magda identifies as a non-binary Sephardic Jew and decided that a surgery to sharpen their jawline in addition to body-sculpting to reduce hip size was necessary to obtain a more androgynous appearance that would be most comfortable. They cashed out their retirement account to pay for the procedures.

SELF ASSESSMENT

1. These are resources I know about for gender affirming hormone therapy in my area:

....
....
....
....
....
....

2. These are questions I want to find the answers to regarding gender affirming hormone providers in my area:

....
....
....
....
....
....

3. These are the surgeons I know of in my region and the surgeries each one offers:

....
....
....
....
....
....

4. These are questions I will find answers to about the surgeons in my area:

    . . . .

    . . . .

    . . . .

    . . . .

    . . . .

    . . . .

    . . . .

5. Here are some financial resources or ideas about getting medical gender affirming services funded for my clients:

    . . . .

    . . . .

    . . . .

    . . . .

    . . . .

    . . . .

    . . . .

6. I'm confident about assisting clients with preparing for surgery.

    Y   **N**

7. These are words I need to familiarize myself with and practice saying so I can talk to my clients about sexual health if applicable:

....

....

....

....

....

....

8. Here are supplies or resources I will have onsite regarding sexual and reproductive health for trans clients:

....

....

....

....

....

....

....

Scenarios

You are working with a 23-year-old Dominican man of trans experience who recently attempted suicide, had a terrible time in the hospital due to overhearing transphobic comments by hospital staff, being mis-gendered throughout the stay, and being sexually harassed by one hospital staff member, and was recently released. He lives with three roommates and works as a delivery driver. The hospital prescribed medication for depression and diagnosed him with borderline personality disorder, but your client does not believe medication is the right approach to healing for him and does not agree with this Diagnostic & Statistical Manual concept of mental illness. You also know that trans folx tend to be over-diagnosed with this disorder. Your clinic has a foundation that provides grant funding to individuals seeking medical transition services. He is applying for funding and also seeking a letter from you for chest masculinization surgery which is supposed to state that his mental health symptoms are "reasonably well controlled." What is your approach? What community resources do you share with the client? Is your writing of the letter connected to the rest of your care and work with the client? Why, or why not? Who would you consult with? What alternative to hospitalization do you collaborate on in safety planning?

. . . .

. . . .

. . . .

. . . .

. . . .

. . . .

. . . .

. . . .

. . . .

. . . .

. . . .

. . . .

. . . .

. . . .

. . . .

You are working with a 37-year-old white non-binary femme who has developed chronic pain in the past couple of years and is having to adapt to living life with more restrictions and less physical ability than before. Occasionally they have to stay in bed and miss work, and they cannot climb stairs or walk long distances. Many events they want to attend don't have accessible entrances or seating, which has caused feelings of isolation. They have had two surgeries in the past two years to attempt to reduce the pain, with limited success. They are polyamorous and are struggling to figure out how their sexual experiences need to change as a person with disabilities, and how to talk about what they need and want from sex now with their partners. Write out a possible conversation that might happen with this person in therapy:

CHAPTER 6

Working with Trans Elders

In the "trans-only" community room at the conference, she sat next to me. Both of us with hair in various stages of silver, she with more wrinkles, looking gorgeous in a purple skirt and jacket and red glossy nails. As we bonded over the free lunch of fruit and cheese, hard rolls, one of those veggie trays and chocolate chip cookies, she looked at me and said "Baby, you don't know what we went through. Let me tell you a story..." (Tavi Hawn)

The elders I work with are in many different situations. Some transitioned years ago and hold historical community knowledge of the way things were decades ago. Others are just starting on the journey to outwardly express and tell others who they truly are at the age of 65 or 72. These different situations can also mean people are in very different financial circumstances. Elders who came out in their youth may live in poverty due to experiences of life-long discrimination. This is even more the case for elders of color. Those I work with, who are just coming out in their 60s and 70s, often have spouses, adult children, and may be entering retirement from life-long careers. In fact, 70 percent of trans elders report delaying coming out in order to maintain employment (James *et al.* 2016). The needs and desires of elders can vary based on where they are with life experiences.

In one qualitative study with TPOC elders, 8 out of 9 participants shared that race had impacted their lives more than gender identity and that race and gender could not be separated in their lives. One elder said "Everything from my point of view is about race, about ethnicity. Access to funds, access to resources, the creation of wealth, the transfer of wealth, generationally. It's all related" (Rodriguez 2016, p.33).

Elders I meet who started their transition years ago were often involved in community building at that time, starting support groups, organizing for rights, mentoring younger TGNC2S people. Many talk to me about feeling isolated now. Some say they don't feel the need to attend support groups anymore, or want to meet people based on shared interests versus identity. Others say they want community, but feel that trans communities they find are very youth-oriented without respect or valuing of elders' lived experiences and wisdom or desire to learn their local history. One elder I worked with couldn't attend groups or events for elders because they were held during the day. "They assume we can all retire, but I still have to work," she said. Many elders I've worked with had trouble attending evening meetings due to not having transportation and needing help navigating a new location in the dark. In the qualitative study mentioned above, another elder said "I'll tell you one thing, our community is so separated...so ununited. Everyone's got their own agenda to fulfill...we have too many leaders... in the 60's, we were Blacks, Asians, Mexicans, and Whites all together fighting for the same thing! And nowadays, everyone's got their own little cliques... So it doesn't bring the community any stronger" (Rodriguez 2016, p.34). They can feel attacked for holding beliefs or language that is viewed as outdated, or being physically unable to engage in direct action, without being in a reciprocal relationship and without younger folx taking on caring responsibilities for the elders. Elders with specific cultural knowledge and practices may feel that younger trans and Two Spirits are often not willing to spend time or be inconvenienced to acquire teachings, history, and medicine. Elders turning to LGBTQ+ centers for assistance sometimes find an absence of programming and resources for gender non-conforming elders. People living in rural areas or suburbs of cities may not have supportive local resources or ability to travel for community and resources. Some elders speak about "survivor's guilt," having lost so many trans community members to murder and suicide along the way.

Housing

Safe housing is a need of many trans elders. Some find themselves trying to survive with just Social Security or disability. Many trans elders have been under-employed or unemployed for a long time due to discrimination. TPOC have generally been much more impacted economically by discrimination; for example, American Indians face 36 percent job loss due to transgender status, followed by Blacks and Latina/os at 32 percent and 30 percent (Grant *et al.* 2011). Others may still be working, but have been estranged from biological family, have no children, and have chosen family that they believe are not willing or able to financially care for them when they have to stop working. In fact, while many elders in the general population can and do rely on biological family for caregiving, over 50 percent of trans elders report being estranged from their families of origin (Filar 2015). Fear of homelessness in older age is a reality. Fear of going into assisted living facilities that are transphobic is real. Many would rather anything happen than have to be in a nursing home where they may experience physical and emotional abuse, as well as refusal to acknowledge their identity or give access to gender affirming items. At the same time, long term care that might be needed is expensive and beyond the finances of many trans individuals. Other trans elders have been outright denied admission to nursing homes needed for medical care. Fear of Alzheimer's and dementia is also talked about, due to worries about whether the person will lose their memory of their identity or will be helpless to advocate for themselves within a transphobic environment.

Some cities now have subsidized LGBTQ+ elder housing communities; activists are working to improve legislation and care in assisted living facilities and shelters; some trans elders create communal housing situations; and some LGBTQ+ young adults and trans elders are living as roommates. For ways to get involved in this work, you could contact Services and Advocacy for Gay, Lesbian, Bisexual and Transgender Elders (SAGE) about their National LGBT Elder Housing Initiative.

Healthcare

In one study, 40 percent of trans adults reported fear of accessing healthcare services (Fredriksen-Goldsen *et al.* 2014). This number increased with internalized stigma and experiences of victimization. This led to both poorer physical and mental health outcomes compared to the cisgender LGB participants. Trans adults in the study also had higher rates of military service than cis LGB participants. This correlated with higher rates of post-traumatic stress disorder (PTSD) as well. At a time in life when most of us are experiencing more health needs and physical challenges, it can become even more frightening to try to access care and more difficult to find informed, appropriate care. Lack of access to medical care increases for people of color. In fact, 31 percent of Black, 28 percent of Latino/a, and 25 percent of American Indian transgender people are uninsured, as compared to 17 percent of their white counterparts (Grant *et al.* 2011).

Word of mouth can be really useful in helping your clients connect to trusted healthcare resources. By that, I mean word of mouth amongst the trans community. Notice the difference between providers recommending themselves as "friendly" or "affirming" versus trans folx recommending providers. There've been times when I knew a trans person working as a certified nursing assistant (CAN) and could connect elders who needed in home care with this person, as well as a trans employee at a nursing home, so I could recommend that center as a safer assisted living facility, based on what I knew from the employee. You can learn which healthcare clinics and staff people report good experiences with, versus negative experiences.

You may want to find out about affirming case workers who can assist your clients with applying for Medicare, Medicaid, disability, or social security benefits. In the absence of a caseworker, you should assist clients with this process. Medicare covers routine preventative care for all people regardless of gender marker, hormone therapy (may need to show medical necessity), and gender affirming surgery. This coverage is determined on an individual basis according to Standards of Care. If coverage is denied by Medicare, clients can appeal. There is a special CMS (Center for Medicare and Medicaid) billing code (condition code 45) which may help with filing claims, instructing the computer system to ignore assumed "gender mis-matches" (National Center for Transgender Equality 2014).

While a large body of research is still lacking regarding the use of gender affirming hormone therapy in elders, what we do know at this point is that trans people using HRT seem to face higher risk of cardiovascular disease, liver disease, and diabetes, all treatable with proper access to healthcare, but life threatening for those without (Persson 2009).

Sometimes a client may want you to help screen healthcare providers. You can call them and ask questions like "How many transgender patients have you worked with?," "How are patients greeted by staff?," "Have your staff been trained in working with trans and gender non-conforming people?," "How do you ask about gender identity, pronouns and what body parts a person has pertaining to the reason they're seeking medical care?," "Will my client be able to designate where they would be most comfortable rooming here?"

Your client may also wish to work with non-Western healers in addition to, or instead of, engaging in the Western medical model. It's important to respect that your client may prefer their cultural medicines and healing ceremonies and to assist in decreasing any barriers to accessing these.

Your work will need to be trauma informed, as many of our elders have experienced anti-trans abuse and harassment, in addition to other types of trauma in their lives.

Legal assistance

Many trans elders do not have legal documents in place to protect themselves as they age. There are many, many reasons for this, with lack of privilege being one. It's important to talk with trans elders about their desires and plans in case of accident, health crisis, dementia, and so on. Some elders may fear that hostile relatives may try to intervene and take guardianship of them, denying access to their loved ones and freedom. Your clients may want someone they trust immensely for a Power of Attorney, someone who would take over financial decisions. They may want Advanced Care Directives, designating medical wishes and that gender identity must be respected in medical settings. An elder may want a Living Will, designating their wishes about life-sustaining procedures. They can also create Visitation Directives, naming people they do or do not want allowed to visit if they are in a hospital or long term care facility. They can also identify a Pre-Need Guardian, so that the court will not appoint any other person as legal guardian if they are incapacitated. These are not scenarios any of us enjoy imagining and they can create a lot of fear in elders. Knowing that there are legal documents that are harder to ignore can give some peace of mind. Along with these legal needs, elder clients may need help with identity documents, veteran's benefits, immigration rights, and so on.

Another reason to assist your clients with having legal documents in place is due to elder abuse. Forge's Transgender Aging Network did a survey in 2007, documenting all types of abuse experienced by transgender elders (Cook-Daniels & Munson 2010). They found many instances of financial abuse (by family members and sometimes even younger trans individuals), physical and sexual abuse, spiritual/religious abuse, and abandonment (being cut off from children and grandchildren).

Some law groups, law schools, and LGBTQ+ centers occasionally hold free legal clinics for trans elders. You can research whether anyone in your area does this. You can also check out the Trans Legal Services Network Directory compiled by the National Center for Transgender Equality (n.d.).

Social connection

Trans, Two Spirit, or gender non-conforming elders can sometimes feel lonely and isolated. Some may have built a community for themselves over time and maintained it, but others may have lost most community members and partners already, have had to move around a lot, have experienced exclusion from cultural community or biological family, do not know how to locate other TGNC2S people in their area, do not have any local resources for aging TGNC2S people, or have not prioritized staying in community with other LGBTQ+ people or other Two Spirits. In terms of getting out to meet with other folx, finances, transportation, or health concerns can be barriers. Suicidal ideation can increase for elders who are isolated.

You can find out what type of connection would be meaningful for your client. Some elders want to learn more about online communities to use the internet to increase connection. Others may want to connect one on one with another person or at events or groups. In the absence of formal supports, you may decide to use your office or organization as a location for an elder support or social group, or create a system where TGNC2S elders can leave their contact information for another elder to take, or you may create a visitation program where TGNC2S youth go and regularly spend time with an elder in their home or nursing facility.

You can share with clients or keep in the communal space at your practice location *To Survive on This Shore*, a photography and interview project of TGNC2S elders over age 65 by Jess Dugan and Dr. Vanessa Fabbre (2018).

Finding meaning and creating legacy

It's important that all elders feel their value and have meaning in their lives. In Western, colonized culture it can seem that only those who are constantly "productive," "working," and engaging in capitalism have value. It's necessary for communities to give honor to trans and Two Spirit elders and seek out their wisdom, gifts, talents, and ensure that their roles are recognized and they are not cast aside or ignored. Elders may struggle sometimes to see their worth or to see how they continue to have importance and meaning when their physical or mental abilities may have changed and they may feel the worlds they are attempting to exist in are so disparate. Part of your work with an elder may be assisting them in not accepting a devaluing of themselves and maintaining their vitality and life force. You may ask about the person's view of the legacy they will leave—what do they want their legacy to be and how do they see themselves fulfilling that now? Some elders want to write, create art, run for office, mentor youth, pursue medical interventions that were out of reach when younger, engage in activism, perform, teach.

Elders new in transition

I've worked with many, many elders who knew they were transgender at a young age but buried the awareness due to physical and verbal punishment for attempting to express their gender, or social messaging about it being "abnormal." I've talked with a number of trans elders who experienced severe physical and emotional abuse in early childhood when parents or caregivers observed gender non-conforming behaviors or expression. Some were even sexually assaulted by fathers or other family members when discovered dressing in feminine clothing, as "corrective rape." These children often did not tell anyone that this happened until coming out as trans in their sixties or seventies. Some developed coping mechanisms for gender identity-related abuse, such as compartmentalization, intense repression, fragmented identity, or dissociation. Others knew they felt "something was different" but had no knowledge of gender non-conforming people and therefore didn't make the connection to their gender identity until much later. Some elders have waited for parents or other family members to die before coming out, or had made a promise to a relative or spouse that they would never change their body. Trauma recovery work is often part of therapy with elders. People who start some type of gender transition in their sixties and seventies are sometimes more financially stable, but may fear they risk losing a spouse, relationships with adult children, and, potentially, their job. Families will be transitioning and this is often a public process. Everyone's identities may be viewed differently. Some talk openly about the fact of losing privileges they were given by living a cis-hetero-normative life. Some elders I've known during transition have had neighbors tell them to stay away from their children and have lost friends they've had for years. Some may not be allowed to be around grandchildren. I've heard trans elders say that the resources they had in a previous life are no longer available, while they are navigating a "starting over" late in life. However, a lot of these elders have told me they want their last season of life to be lived fully as themselves and are tired of having to hide or deny who they are. Medical transition at this age is possible, though there may be additional health risks. I have known some elder clients to have blood clots from hormone therapy or to need close monitoring of cholesterol, blood pressure, and so on while on hormone therapy. The method of delivery is usually not oral for elder clients. Surgeries may carry higher risk as well and this information and planning is part of informed consent. Family members of these clients may also need support and aging clients may need referrals to relationship counseling or legal services.

Many of my elder clients who are transitioning express excitement and feelings of renewed youthfulness as they take steps in affirming their gender. Some will want referrals for hair removal, make-up lessons, vocal coaching, support during shopping for clothing, information on body-shaping gear, and so on. I've been able to witness aging trans folx who were isolated and lonely, sometimes unemployed or living with unsupportive family members, become very social, creative, expressive, and active as they transition, demonstrating determination and resourcefulness.

SELF ASSESSMENT

1. These are three challenges facing TGNC2S elders:

....

....

....

....

....

....

....

....

2. This is a place that offers case management for trans elders, or these are the resources I have to assist elder clients with basic needs:

....

....

....

....

....

....

....

....

3. This is an example of a legal document a trans elder might need assistance with:

....

....

....

....

....

....

....

....

4. These are some ways I could work collaboratively with an elder to increase social connection and meaning in their lives:

....

....

....

....

....

....

....

....

Scenarios

You are working with a Korean American elder who is seeking help in understanding their gender identity and alleviating decades-long gender dysphoria. This elder lives with a cisgender female spouse, an adult daughter, and a cousin who has cancer and is being cared for by the family members. Your client works for an insurance company and has had a middle class lifestyle. Discuss some things that might come up, approaches you might take, or resources you need to explore:

....
....
....
....
....
....
....
....
....
....
....
....

You are working with a Chippewa Two Spirit elder who came out in the 1980s and experienced a negative reaction which led to leaving community and family behind for some years. This elder worked to create Two Spirit gatherings and also advocated to raise awareness of missing and murdered Indigenous women and Two Spirits. Now your client will be returning to tribal homelands to live. She has been dealing with arthritis and hip problems and has increasingly limited mobility. What would you consider in your work? What do you need to know or learn? What might come up and what resources might your client want?

....
....
....

....

....

....

....

....

....

....

....

....

CHAPTER 7

Trans on Both Sides of the Couch

When the Therapist Is Trans Identified

In the few books that exist on providing therapy to trans folx, I've never been able to read something that was addressed to trans therapists. I read research and books about us, hear about workshops cis providers are leading about trans issues, but rarely get to hear us speak to one another. I believe the assumption is usually that none of us work in this field. I've had the privilege and joy of being in some circles with trans identified providers: therapists, attorneys, researchers, bodyworkers, teachers. And those were some life-giving conversations for me. So, this chapter's for all of you.

This circle, it holds ME, it holds US. The place where I'm known, I'm seen, pronouns used, no jokes like "'she' or call me whatever, haha," where my faggy ass can paint my lips and nails and prance around, and you know it still doesn't mean I'm only "woman." This circle, where I can be femme and butch at once and sing a high alto and low tenor and no one here will call me m'am after. The gift of my Being, keeping the balance, is recognized, is honored, is valued, after being told I'm "going to hell/eternally lost/it's really not loving to Love you." This circle, where I can two step the way that my body wants, where I CAN be loved, be touched in ways that feel good, where Spirit blesses us too, where our magic is truly divine. This circle keeps me alive. S'gi (thank you). (Tavi Hawn)

Transference and counter-transference

When we share some identity, our clients may have assumptions about who we are, what we believe, what we like and don't, and so on. Sometimes those assumptions are right and other times we may find that our client is projecting something of their own emotions or experiences onto us. We then decide whether or not to address this and how it may impact the therapeutic relationship.

At the same time, we may have counter-transference with a client. We may notice a certain reaction or feeling that happens often when a certain client is with us. This may be information about how others also experience the client and that could be useful for therapy. Other times we may need to notice things about ourselves: Are we ignoring what needs to be challenged in session because we find our client attractive? How do we handle it when a client tells us they are attracted to us? Are we laughing at our client's jokes but overlooking their symptoms of depression? Do we want to be liked and have our client tell everyone in the community how great a therapist we are, so much that we don't ask reflective questions or point out behaviors that are causing our client heartache?

Dealing with these issues can be challenging with someone you may also share community with. But, if we handle the subjects carefully, it can be a powerful moment of learning in therapy and can strengthen the relationship. Then there are times that we need to reflect something we're observing to a trans or GNC client and our client might react with anger and even terminate therapy with us. That can bring up insecurity or worry that whatever the client may say about their experience will hurt our other relationships in our community because we know we cannot respond or even acknowledge that this person was a client.

There are some instances of this that can be unique to a trans therapist, or queer trans therapist, working within community.

In conversations with peers and groups of trans colleagues, some examples of things that might need to be processed in session or consulted about are things like:

- "A client keeps telling me they want their body to look like mine, or that life would be easier if their body looked like mine."

- "Clients ask me what medical interventions I've had and why or why not."

- "A client said to me 'identifying as non-binary is taking the easy way out.'"

- "My client's parent keeps using the wrong pronouns for me in front of my client as a passive aggressive way to hurt my client.'"

- "My client's family tells them they are sick and need help because of their gender identity and it can be hard to hear in session, thinking about how my own family responded too."

There are also things that can happen that are hurtful in session with another trans person. For instance, my binary trans clients can mis-gender me more than cisgender clients do. This causes sadness and still sometimes surprises me.

We may experience microaggressions and sometimes outright harassment during the professional trainings we offer, and may need to be in community, access our own support, or be alone to practice our own healing afterwards. I've had people direct anger at me during a training because they're being asked to consider things about gender they haven't before, including how and why we assign gender to infants or fetuses. I've known of a colleague who had an attendee read a religious text out loud over him while giving the training and refuse to stop, so my colleague had to just end the training. I took a break from doing these trainings for a time until I felt ready to handle these reactions again. I make plans now for how I want to spend my time directly after giving a training and who I want to talk to about how things went.

Shit, this community is small

Speaking of community, one of the biggest challenges in being trans or Two Spirit and working with your people, is that, because communities can be small, even in cities, you most likely will have overlapping relationships or at least interact more socially with clients than other therapists might. I learned to talk about this early on with clients, but there are still times I need to consult with a trans colleague about the most ethical way to handle complicated situations or connections. At the same time, we have to recognize that professional codes of ethics were not created with folx like us and communities like ours in mind. I've heard of various ways my trans colleagues try to navigate working within community, but, generally, the common theme is communicating as openly and specifically as possible throughout the therapeutic relationship. You can start this way and may need to re-visit as relationships of your client change, as you find out new information that relates to you, and so on. There are times that, even with consultation, I've later felt that the way I communicated about navigating social situations with a client was not the most effective or as transparent as it could have been. Sometimes we have to apologize and repair the relationship. Other times we have to know when to refer out for the client's benefit or for our own.

Here are some examples of challenges I've heard from other trans colleagues or experienced myself:

- "A client and I just realized we went on a date with the same person recently."

- "I have to inform my client that I perform drag/burlesque/comedy/attend play parties, etc. to discuss boundaries and feelings that could impact the therapy relationship."

- "A client and I realized we are going to be working on a community organizing project together."

- "A client came in and got their hair cut next to me and it was hard to navigate conversation with my barber, knowing my client could hear."

- "My client and I are both part of a local trans advocacy group."

- "My client will tell friends they see me for therapy, then in a social setting a friend will say 'hey, so and so told me about something funny you said in session' and I have to say I can't confirm that I know who or what they are speaking about."

Some therapists who really want distance from clients can struggle with feeling like they can't have their own community or support. Sometimes these therapists try to create some space by working in a town outside of where they live or by varying their caseload more, so they are not just working with gender non-conforming people. Other times, it really can feel isolating, especially if your colleagues are only or primarily cis, straight people.

Acknowledging power and privilege differences even when trans identity is shared

Trans/Two Spirit identified clinicians: We have some level of privilege if we are providing mental health services that we had to attend school or receive training in order to do and/or are paid for our work. We can practice in a way to minimize the power differential in the healing relationship, but we have to acknowledge that it exists. We can talk about this openly with clients and how it feels to have that power difference in the room, with someone you may be in community with as well.

There may be a difference in race or ethnic identity between you and your client and this may need to be talked about as well and needs to be something we're comfortable and able to talk about as part of the therapy relationship. If you experience less (or no) racism compared to your client, you can talk about what that is like for them and what they are and aren't comfortable sharing with you. If you experience more racism than your client, you may have a boundary, for example, a white client processing their own feelings of guilt or confusion about what is and is not racist, and may need to communicate this upfront or in the moment.

You can discuss whether your client might be more comfortable working with someone of a shared racial or ethnic identity or heritage and have trusted referrals on hand. You may need to suggest that you are not the person a client processes certain things with and have resources specific to those things as well to share.

There may be a range of other privileges you might hold that a client doesn't: class, ability, citizenship status, and so on. These are things that can be acknowledged and talked about in terms of the therapeutic relationship.

These differences can also impact the relationships we might have with other trans identified colleagues. We might have trans colleagues who don't talk about race, who aren't trying to leverage their own privileges to expand the circle, and who are content to live with whatever level of access they've achieved while not working for collective liberation. Sometimes this can feel more lonely than not having trans colleagues at all. We may have to figure out how to have challenging conversations and dialogue.

Whatever privileges we do hold, we need to be asking ourselves how we use those to create more access, to provide better care, to support various movements to increase rights, equity, and freedom for people without the privileges we have. None of us are exempt from this work and responsibility because we are marginalized in some other way. We may need to rest and heal and be held in relation to oppressions we do experience, while not allowing ourselves to withdraw and hide in whatever privilege we have. There may be seasons of life where we need more support and holding and seasons where we are more active in the struggle for justice. But opting out entirely from examination, learning, growth, and advocacy is not an ethical option.

Seeking your own professional and social support

If you work with other trans folx and know the other trans identified healers in your area, you know it can be really, really hard to find your own support. What if you want to be in a large Facebook group for support for TGNC2S people who are trying to conceive or have had a miscarriage and know that you have clients who are in the group? What if you are coming out about your own gender identity and want social support, but have clients in all the local support groups? What if you want to work with a therapist or other kind of healer but with someone who's outside of your close circle? What if you want to attend a relationship or sex related workshop but are worried you'll be there with clients? What if you want to hire an administrator or peer support staff from your trans community but wonder about navigating friendship/community relationship and a supervisory role?

These are questions and conversations I've had with so many folx now. It's such a challenge that friends have shared ideas, suggestions, and resources with me, and I've done the same with them. Some people have sought professional help outside of their local area through video or text services. Some have decided to prioritize a specialist in a certain skill set or healing focus over a provider with trans identity. I did that once myself to do a certain type of trauma recovery work, but ended up quitting after my therapist just couldn't get my pronouns and gender identity right after multiple discussions. I have a friend who needed trauma work and tried for two years with a cis therapist to get their pronouns and gender right before giving up. Some only use non-Western healers of various kinds rather than utilizing psychotherapy. Others attend any support group or workshop they want to and inform clients that they'll be there and want their participation to be respected and confidential, or they join or attend and listen/observe but don't personally share if clients are present. Sadly, I've heard some folx say they just don't have community or their own support because it's too complicated with their work. My encouragement is that we all deserve support in whatever form we want and believe in. We may have to get creative about how we seek and receive it, but we're allowed to be human, to be social and relational, and to need our own healing.

Working together with trans colleagues and community to build power

Something that also often comes up in the few spaces I get to be in with other trans providers is what to do about "the allies." I've heard and experienced now, so many instances of cis folx identifying themselves as "specialists" or "experts" on trans or Two Spirit care, not hiring trans folx or trans folx of color, competing for grant funding with trans led organizations for work with trans folx (and when winning the funding, not sharing it or giving it to trans led groups), refusing to pay for trainings led by trans people and even leading trainings on trans folx themselves, leading "support groups" for trans folx, asking TGNC2S people to do *all* the free labor ("I need resources/topics/suggestions/education/consultation/panelists..."), starting their own grant foundation for transition services for trans folx instead of just donating their money to an existing trans led organization that is already doing the work, and so on. I've had the supervisor of a large "gender clinic" straight up tell me "We don't prioritize hiring transgender people, we prioritize hiring the most qualified people." A space with that mentality is absolutely not a space for us, and yet some of us will still have to access care in them. Oh yeah, and there are the large "professional" bodies that want to charge trans people exorbitant fees to earn "certifications" in working with trans people or be able to fly to a fancy conference every year. What are we gonna do about that, y'all?

I hope that my people can recognize that we don't have to collectively accept these things. It's sad when sometimes I see that we've been conditioned to accept crumbs, tokenization and undervaluing. I hope that we can see the difficulty in accessing education, opportunities, spaces, positions, funding, and employment as a systemic issue, a result of structural oppression. I hope we can acknowledge the mental toll of trying to get and keep a job without matching documents, references that only know our dead names, in places that mis-gender us daily, *and that this does not make us less "qualified," "skilled," or whatever the fuck.* Regardless of what cis folx might verbalize, they are not "allies" if they are not actively challenging these things both within, and outside of, their own spheres of existence and influence. A cis white queer woman or cis gay man of color, for example, who does not *actively* work to increase access to education and employment, to shift leadership within organizations and change employment requirements, to have representative staffing, to give up a seat on the panel, on the committee, the paid position, to spend more time addressing anti-trans bias and exclusion in their circles than profiting from work with trans people, can harm our communities by maintaining structural/institutional oppression, all the while with a rainbow sticker or trans flag on their door.

I want to encourage us to work together to refuse to do that free labor anymore and to ask our cis "allies" why they are speaking on our behalf for free or for pay. I want to embolden my trans relatives to put the agencies, clinics, centers, organizations, commissions, and festivals on notice when they continue to make decisions for our communities without meaningful representation. I know we're tired, at least a lot of the time I feel tired (and I'm 40 now, so I have definitely felt my energy decline lately). Still, let's dream. What can we create in our neighborhood, in a region of our state, in our city that's missing? If resources that we want don't exist, how can we make them? If service providers won't honor the wisdom and lived experiences of TGNC2S people, how can we create those services ourselves? We're artists, writers, dancers, singers, lovers, geeks and nerds, planners, good cooks, emergency medical technicians, doulas, healers, teachers, organizers, and so much more. This earth needs us in order to stay in balance. When we know what we want and what we are on the journey to creating, then we can ask those who believe they are "allies" for specific types of support if we desire any kind of help or assistance.

SELF REFLECTION CHECKLIST

1. An experience of transference or counter-transference I've had is:

. . . .

. . . .

. . . .

. . . .

. . . .

. . . .

. . . .

2. Ideas for how to navigate community and possibly multiple roles or relationships:

. . . .

. . . .

. . . .

. . . .

. . . .

. . . .

. . . .

3. These are some of my privileges:

. . . .

. . . .

. . . .

. . . .

. . . .

....

....

4. These are some ways I can leverage these in the service of trans liberation and building equitable communities:

....

....

....

....

....

....

....

5. Here are some ideas of ways I can get my own support:

....

....

....

....

....

....

....

6. Here are ways I can advocate for myself and more marginalized TGNC2S folx:

....

....

....

....

. . . .

. . . .

7. Here are some dreams I have for what I'd love to create with and for trans community:

. . . .

. . . .

. . . .

. . . .

. . . .

. . . .

. . . .

CHAPTER 8

Ethical Guidelines

There are a couple of professional organizations that offer us ethical codes and practice guidelines to apply to our work with TGNC2S populations.

NASW Code of Ethics (Workers 2008)
Code 1.05 Cultural Awareness and Social Diversity

This standard speaks to the need for providers to be life-long learners of various cultures, to take an interest in an individual client's culture and take responsibility for educating themselves about that culture. It is necessary to engage in this learning in order to provide appropriate care. Providers should recognize the various social identities held by a client, which of those identities may lead to experiences of oppression, and how accessing services might be affected or informed by one's multiple identities.

Code 6.04 Social and Political Action

Social workers, whether in clinical practice, direct service care, or more macro-level work, should understand the impact of policy and legislation on the most marginalized peoples. Providers of all types should engage in advocacy and activism to address injustice at the policy and legislative level. Social workers should take actions to ensure that practices and policies address inequity and create a more just and free society. Providers must prevent exploitation and discrimination of any class, group, or identity. These ethical standards call us to action both at the micro and macro levels of work. Whatever our practice setting, we are all held to these standards if we are engaging in ethical work.

American Psychological Association's 2015 Practice Guidelines (APA 2015)

These guidelines start from a place of acknowledging that there are multiple genders, speaking to the historical context of colonization, Westernization, and violent erasure of other genders, and the medical stigmatization of gender non-conforming people. The guidelines encourage psychologists to understand the difference between gender identity and sexual orientation. Clinicians are also asked to recognize the ways that various identities can intersect, connect, relate, and influence life experiences. Self reflection and awareness of one's own attitudes and beliefs about gender may affect the work are encouraged. The guidelines also require psychologists to acknowledge the ways that stigma and violence affect the health and overall wellbeing of TGNC2S people. It's important that clinicians can view symptoms as typical and reasonable responses to a culture or mainstream society that is oppressive. Psychologists are asked to consider various needs and experiences through the lifespan, as well as institutional barriers to meeting those needs. Practitioners are encouraged to seek to decrease barriers to informed, affirming care. These guidelines also recommend that psychologists improve training of students and new practitioners in trans affirming and knowledgeable care (American Psychological Association 2015).

Ethical decision-making models

At times providers will have questions about the most ethical approach or response to a complicated situation. Some people find it helpful to have a model to use to carefully think through scenarios and situations and ensure intentional reflection. Here are two models developed by social workers that you can use or that may help you to develop another model that works for you.

1. The first is a question-based model.

Can I clearly define competing ethical principles in this situation? If so, what are they? If not, do I need to consult with an appropriate other to clarify my thoughts? Are issues of culture involved here? (*consultation; cultural sensitivity*). If I determine that this is an ethical dilemma, where am I placed within it? Is it my role to make a decision, or should this situation be referred to someone with higher authority? (*accountability*). Is this situation familiar to me or do I need new knowledge? Can I draw on past experience or on what I have learnt from work in other contexts? (*critical reflection*). (McAuliffe and Chenoweth 2008, pp.43–44)

2. The second uses an acronym to help remember steps to take.

- E: Examine relevant personal, societal, cultural, agency, client and professional values

- T: Think about the ethical standards that your professional organization and state regulations reference that pertain to the dilemma, as well as related case laws and legislation

- H: Hypothesize about the outcome of each option

- I: Identify who will benefit and who will be harmed *in keeping with social work's commitment to the most vulnerable*

- C: Consult with colleagues and supervisor. (Congress 2000, pp.10–11)

I'm going to provide one ethical dilemma here. Please use the first model to come up with your action steps.

A white Jewish cisgender mother brings in a 16-year-old adolescent transfeminine client. The parent tells you on the phone beforehand that a large gender clinic in a nearby city had recommended that the teen start gender affirming hormone therapy, but that the mother thinks they made the decision too quickly and she thinks her teen is just "looking for a reason for being depressed and is hoping that transitioning will be like a magic happy pill." She tells you the teen is withholding and secretive and that you probably won't get any information from her. The client's mother does use her pronouns correctly on the phone. You meet with the young person who talks very openly in the session and explains that her depression started a couple of years ago when she realized she was transgender but was upset by the realization and at first did not want to be trans. After she came to more acceptance about it, she came out to her mother and father who are divorced and have joint custody. She feels her mother has had a very hard time accepting her identity and her father is more actively supportive. From the teen, you hear that the mother frequently snaps at the young person, insists that they spend time together but then lectures her throughout dinner or on walks together. The young person reports that she felt hopeful when the clinic prescribed hormones and thought she would be medically transitioning but in the past two months, when her mother refused to fill the prescription, she has at times been suicidal. She believes her mother never plans to allow a medical transition, but will not come out and admit that she will continue to block it.

Please answer the questions from Model 1:

. . . .

. . . .

. . . .

. . . .

. . . .

. . . .

. . . .

. . . .

. . . .

. . . .

I'm going to provide another ethical dilemma here. Please use the second model to come up with your action steps.

You have been working with a 25-year-old undocumented Indigenous client from Bolivia. She speaks English as a second language and tells you that she is a woman of transgender experience. You assisted her with getting a scholarship from a foundation which allowed her to receive a gender affirming surgery. She had a significant complication from surgery, which the hospital and surgeon have taken little responsibility for, and basically stated that she must have done something wrong in following her recovery protocol. She has no family here but did have a friend who came by to help her the first few days after surgery. You requested a meeting with the hospital staff and surgeon but they didn't grant the meeting. You think that she is displaying trauma symptoms now, but she denies this and says that she has been feeling like dying because the complication happened and now she needs a revision surgery. In supervision, your director told you that he thinks she is suicidal and needs to be hospitalized. He says this is a liability if she impulsively acts on these statements and the program did not hospitalize her.

Write out your thoughts based on the ETHIC model:

. . . .

. . . .

. . . .

. . . .

. . . .

. . . .

. . . .

. . . .

. . . .

. . . .

. . . .

Here is one last dilemma to think through.

You are working with a 35-year-old Black gender non-conforming adult who uses they/them pronouns. They have a two-year-old child and their ex-wife has taken the child and moved out of state. Your client has gone to visit once but it was difficult since they don't have a car. There was no formal custody agreement when they separated a few months ago. Now your client's ex-wife has filed for full custody with no visitation rights. She is using your client's gender transition and mental health diagnosis of post-traumatic stress disorder with dissociative episodes, due to experiencing hate crimes, as basis for her claims that they are unfit to parent. Since the custody suit, your client has been having panic attacks and has had to leave work on several occasions. Your client has some friends at church who helped financially to obtain a trans affirming family lawyer. You've been told that your records will be subpoenaed and you will likely be called to testify.

Use either decision-making model to work on this.

. . . .

. . . .

. . . .

. . . .

. . . .

. . . .

. . . .

....
....
....
....

Appendix: A Letter to Cis Providers

Dear cis provider

Thank you for taking the time to read this book and work through the reflective exercises. For most people, working in mental health or social work fields means working many hours, often without being compensated for the value of the work, without much thanks or attention, with many things you can improve on and many things to learn all the time. So I realize that you could be spending this time any number of ways besides reading this. I'm glad you are and your clients will be glad too.

That said, I have some asks of you based on observations over the years. When I give trainings, supervise clinicians, or just have conversations about working with TGNC2S people, a lot of cis providers are focused on their desire to offer services, to "specialize," to give trainings to their staff or colleagues, to "run groups for trans people," and so on. We do need providers to be informed and able to offer culturally relevant care. We need providers who can practice humility. But I'd like to ask cis providers to prioritize some other things first.

1. Speak to the local undergrad and grad schools in your area that train future providers. Ask how they

recruit trans students and gender non-conforming students of color. Ask how many trans students they are admitting and also how many trans or Two Spirit instructors and faculty they have hired. Ask what their curriculum is on training students in working with LGBTQ+ people. Encourage them to increase representation in the student body and faculty. Ask what policies the school has regarding preferred name on rosters, non-discrimination, gender inclusive housing, how many all gender bathrooms are in each building. Ask your professional association to write a letter with suggestions for improvement.

2. Provide a comfortable, affirming place for a trans student to do an internship. Offer *free* clinical supervision to a trans identified provider working towards a license. Offer some *free* or low cost services specifically to TGNC2S people.

3. Insist that your organization (your workplace and professional organization) recruit and hire trans folx into leadership positions, including trans people of color.

4. When approached to do a training on trans identities or populations, instead of accepting, recommend a number of trans folx in the area, who do the same trainings, who could do it. Or ask some trans folx who they recommend or know that might want to do this training. Maybe you can co-train if the trans identified trainer would like.

5. Understand the higher incidences of harm, physical and emotional, enacted on gender non-conforming individuals by police and psychiatric hospitals, and that your client statistically will experience trauma in an emergency room or hospitalization. Commit to creating alternatives to hospitalization and crisis plans that utilize multiple options before

considering involuntary hospitalization or a call to a crisis unit that involves police escort or transport. If you cannot commit to more creative safety plans or cannot influence an agency policy that insists on hospitalization even without immediate, imminent risk, then this should be made very clear to all gender non-conforming patients from first contact, with specific examples of what that person might say or do that could lead to involuntary hospitalization with police escort or being strapped onto a gurney for transport. I have known too many trans folx who have undergone horrific things because a cis provider did not understand the ramifications of psychiatric hospitalization, or was not able to secure a bed in a more affirming location for a patient. There are many articles you can read on alternatives to hospitalization and it is your responsibility to study this, as well as to find out which area hospitals are the least harmful towards trans folx, to know the process in your county and state for whether police are connected to the crisis response unit, whether police transport people to hospitals, whether someone has to go to an emergency room if there are no immediate beds open, and how patients can file complaints if they feel unsafe in a hospital when admitted. This same awareness is needed when thinking about any institution or system your client may encounter (legal, child welfare, etc.) and commitment must be made to go beyond the minimum to limit harm done to trans, gender non-conforming, Two Spirit individuals.

6. Advocate with your state insurance companies to insist on trans inclusive care. Build networks of medical and mental health advocates to work on legislation, as well as placing consumer pressure on the companies. Inquire about your workplace's policy and insist on your company only buy policies that

include all trans health coverage (even if you think there are no trans employees).

7. Support sex worker outreach and harm reduction groups in your area.

8. Donate to trans led foundations and grant making groups.

9. Donate volunteer hours to campaigns for trans rights at the local, state, and federal level.

10. Contact the nearest transgender center or group and ask what type of support might be helpful: providing childcare for meetings, dropping off food for meetings, lending chairs, coordinating clothing donations, making copies of flyers, or anything that is a behind-the-scenes role that takes some labor off of the trans folx. Don't be offended is the answer is "no thanks."

11. Please commit to investing as much time, energy, emotion, and money into doing things like 1–10 as you do in being a paid provider of services to trans folx.

I get nervous when cis providers are telling me they "specialize" in working with trans folx but the trans people they know are their clients. I don't see a lot of accountability to, or genuine involvement with, trans community. This can feel exploitative to the community, even if you are providing a needed service. It can feel like there is Ego or a "savior complex" at the center of the desire to provide paid services if there is no ongoing relationship with trans folx that does not involve exchange of money or positions of power. This is why I'm asking you to commit to some of the above activities.

SELF REFLECTION

1. Here is one action I will take from the list this week:

. . . .

. . . .

. . . .

. . . .

. . . .

. . . .

2. Here is one action I will take from the list in the next six months:

. . . .

. . . .

. . . .

. . . .

. . . .

. . . .

3. Here is one action I will take from the list this year:

. . . .

. . . .

. . . .

. . . .

. . . .

. . . .

4. Here is how I plan to be held accountable:

. . . .

. . . .

. . . .

. . . .

. . . .

. . . .

References

Introduction

Adames, H., Chavez-Duanes, N., Sharma, S., & Roche, M. (2018) "Intersectionality in psychotherapy: The experiences of an AfroLatinx queer immigrant." *Psychotherapy Theory, Research & Practice 55*, 1, 73–79.

Combahee (n.d.) *Combahee River Collective Statement.* Accessed on July 22, 2019 at https://combaheerivercollective.weebly.com/the-combahee-river-collective-statement.html.

Mahony, T.H., Jacob, J., & Hobson, H. (2017) *Women in Canada: A Gender-Based Statistical Report: Women and the Criminal Justice System.* Ottawa: Statistics Canada.

Robbins, C.K. & McGowan, B.L. (2016) "Intersectional perspectives on gender and gender identity development." *New Directions for Student Services 154*, 71–83.

Chapter 1

Adames, H.Y. & Chavez-Dueñas, N.Y. (2017) *Cultural Foundations and Interventions in Latino/a Mental Health: History, Theory, and within Group Differences.* New York: Routledge.

Fisher-Borne, M., Cain, J.M., & Martin, S.L. (2015) "From mastery to accountability: Cultural humility as an alternative to cultural competence." *Social Work Education 34*, 2, 165–181.

McKenzie, M. (2014) *Black Girl Dangerous on Race, Queerness, Class and Gender.* Oakland, CA: BGD Press.

Move to End Violence (September 7, 2016) *Ally or Co-Conspirator: What it means to act in #Insolidarity.* Accessed on August 6, 2019 at www.movetoendviolence.org/blog/ally-co-conspirator-means-act-insolidarity.

Parham, T.A., White, J.L., & Ajamu, A. (1999) *The Psychology of Blacks.* Upper Saddle River, NJ: Prentice Hall.

Tervalon, M. & Murray-Garcia, J. (1998) "Cultural humility versus cultural competence: A critical distinction in defining physician training outcomes in multicultural education." *Journal of Health Care for the Poor and Underserved 9*, 2, 117–125.

Chapter 2

Asakura, K. (2016) "It takes a village: Applying a social ecological framework of resilience in working with LGBTQ youth." *Families in Society 97*, 1, 15–22.

Asakura, K. (2019) "Extraordinary acts to 'show up': Conceptualizing resilience of LGBTQ youth." *Youth & Society 51*, 2, 268–285.

Brave Heart, M.Y.H., Chase, J., Elkins, J., & Altschul, D.B. (2011) "Historical trauma among Indigenous peoples of the Americas: Concepts, research, and clinical considerations." *Journal of Psychoactive Drugs 43*, 4, 282–290.

Briggs, P., Hayes, S., & Changaris, M. (2018) "Somatic Experiencing® informed therapeutic group for the care and treatment of biopsychosocial effects upon a gender diverse identity." *Front Psychiatry 9*, 53.

Case, R. (2016) "Eco-social work and community resilience: Insights from water activism in Canada." *Journal of Social Work 17*, 4, 391–412.

CBC News (2015) "Lasting effects of trauma reaches across generations through DNA." Accessed on August 6, 2019 at www.cbc.ca/radio/unreserved/buffy-sainte-marie-wab-kinew-and-how-dna-remembers-trauma-1.3242375/lasting-effects-of-trauma-reaches-across-generations-through-dna-1.3243897.

DeGruy, J. (2017) *Post-Traumatic Slave Syndrome: America's Legacy of Enduring Injury and Healing.* Portland, OR: Joy Degruy Publications.

Gone, J. (2009) "A community-based treatment for Native American historical trauma: Prospects for evidence-based practice." *Journal of Consulting and Clinical Psychology 77*, 4, 751–762.

Gourneau, J. (2015) *What Is Historical Trauma?* [video] Accessed on July 22, 2019 at https://extension.umn.edu/mental-health/historical-trauma-and-cultural-healing.

Love, D. (2016) "Post-traumatic slave syndrome and intergenerational trauma: Slavery is like curse passing through the DNA of Black people." *Atlanta Black Star,* June 5.

Madsen, D.L. (2008) "On Subjectivity and Survivance: Re-reading Trauma through The Heirs of Columbus and The Crown of Columbus." In G. Vizenor (ed.) *Survivance.* Lincoln, NE: University of Nebraska Press.

Nickerson, M. (2017) "Dismantling Prejudice and Exploring Social Privilege with EMDR Therapy." In M. Nickerson (ed.) *Cultural Competence and Healing Culturally Based Trauma with EMDR Therapy: Innovative Strategies and Protocols.* New York: Springer.

Phillips, G. (2008) "What is healing?—Appropriate public policy responses." Paper for the FaHCSIA Indigenous Healing Forum, Canberra, September 16–17.

Singh, A.A., Hays, D.G., & Watson, L.S. (2011) "Strength in the face of adversity: Resilience strategies of transgender individuals." *Journal of Counseling & Development 89,* 20–27.

Singh, A. & McElroy, V. (2011) "'Just getting out of bed is a revolutionary act': The resilience of transgender people of color who have survived traumatic life events." *Traumatology 17,* 2, 34.

Vizenor, G. (ed.) (2008) *Survivance.* Lincoln, NE: University of Nebraska Press.

Wadden, M. (2006) "The lost generations." *Toronto Star,* November 25.

Walters, K., Mohammed, S., Evans-Campbell, T., Beltrán, R., Chae, D., & Duran B. (2011) "Bodies don't just tell stories, they tell histories: Embodiment of historical trauma among American Indians and Alaska Natives." *Du Bois Review 8,* 1, 179–189.

Wesley-Esquimaux, C. & Smolewski, M. (2004) *Historic Trauma and Aboriginal Health.* Ottawa: Aboriginal Health Foundation.

Chapter 3

Brayboy, D. (2017) "Two spirits, one heart, five genders." *Indian Country Today,* September 7.

Brown, G.R. (2014) "Qualitative analysis of transgender inmates' correspondence: Implications for departments of correction." *Journal of Correctional Health Care 20,* 4, 334–342.

Clark, K., Hughto, J., & Pachankis, J. (2017) "'What's the right thing to do?' Correctional healthcare providers' knowledge, attitudes and experiences caring for transgender inmates." *Social Science & Medicine 193,* 80–89.

Davis, S. (2019) *The Astonishing History of Singular They.* Accessed on August 6, 2019 at www.academicwritingsuccess.com/the-astonishing-history-of-singular-they.

Flentje, A., Leon, A., Carrico, A., Zheng, D., & Dilley, J. (2016) "Mental and physical health among homeless sexual and gender minorities in a major urban US city." *Journal of Urban Health: Bulletin of the New York Academy of Medicine 93,* 6, 997–1009.

Hook, J.N., Davis, D.E., Owen, J., Worthington, E.L., Jr., & Utsey, S.O. (2013) "Cultural humility: Measuring openness to culturally diverse clients." *Journal of Counseling Psychology 60*, 3, 353–366.

Hunt, S. (2016) *An Introduction to the Health of Two-Spirit People: Historical, Contemporary and Emergent Issues.* Prince George, BC: National Collaborating Centre for Aboriginal Health.

Kattari, S.K. & Begun, S. (2017) "On the margins of marginalized: Transgender homelessness and survival sex." *Affilia 32*, 1, 92–103.

Lawler, O. (2018) "What happened to Roxana Hernandez: The trans woman who died in ICE custody?" *The Cut*, December 5.

Mizock, L. & Mueser, K. (2014) "Employment, mental health, internalized stigma, and coping with transphobia among transgender individuals." *Psychology of Sexual Orientation and Gender Diversity 1*, 2, 146–158.

Morales, A., Corbin-Gutierrez, E.E., & Wang, S.C. (2013) "Latino, immigrant, and gay: A qualitative study about their adaptation and transitions." *Journal of LGBT Issues in Counseling 7*, 2, 125–142.

Quintero, D., Cerezo, A., Morales, A., & Rothman, S. (2015) "Supporting Transgender Immigrant Latinas: The Case of Erika." In O.M. Espín & A.L. Dottolo (eds) *Gendered Journeys: Women, Migration and Feminist Psychology.* London: Palgrave Macmillan.

Roscoe, W. (2000) *Changing Ones: Third and Fourth Genders in Native North America.* London: Palgrave MacMillan.

Snorton, C. (2017) *Black on Both Sides.* Minneapolis, MN: University of Minnesota Press.

White Hughto, J.M., Reisner, S.L., & Pachankis, J.E. (2015) "Transgender stigma and health: A critical review of stigma determinants, mechanisms, and interventions." *Social Science & Medicine 147*, 222–231.

Chapter 4

Battle, J. & Ashley, C. (2008) "Intersectionality, heteronormativity, and black lesbian, gay, bisexual, and transgender (LGBT) families." *Black Women, Gender Families 2*, 1, 1–24.

Brännström, M., Johannesson, L., Bokström, H., Kvarnström, M., *et al.* (2014) "Livebirth after uterus transplantation." *The Lancet 385*, 9968, 607–616.

Boss, P. (2004) "Ambiguous loss research, theory, and practice: Reflections after 9/11." *Journal of Marriage and Family 66*, 551–566.

dickey, l m., Ducheny, K.M., & Ehrbar, R.D. (2016) "Family creation options for transgender and gender nonconforming people." *Psychology of Sexual Orientation and Gender Diversity 3*, 2, 173–179.

Hines, S. (2006) "Intimate Transitions: Transgender practices of partnering and parenting." *Sociology 40*, 2, 353–371.

Meier, C., Sharp, C., Michonski, J., Babcock, J.C., & Fitzgerald, K. (2013) "Romantic relationships of female-to-male trans men: A descriptive study." *International Journal of Transgenderism 14*, 2, 75–85.

Movement Advancement (2018) *National LGBT Movement Report*. Accessed on July 22, 2019 at http://lgbtmap.org/2018-national-lgbt-movement-report.

Nixon, L. (2013) "The right to (trans) parent: A reproductive justice approach to reproductive rights, fertility, and family-building issues facing transgender people." *William & Mary Journal of Race, Gender, and Social Justice 20*, 1.

Norwood, K. (2013) "Meaning matters: Framing trans identity in the context of family relationships." *Journal of GLBT Family Studies 9*, 2, 152–178.

Platt, L.F. & Bolland, K.S. (2018) "Relationship partners of transgender individuals: A qualitative exploration." *Journal of Social and Personal Relationships 35*, 9, 1251–1272.

Polly, K. & Polly, R.G. (2014) "Our Relationships and Families." In L. Erickson-Schroth (ed.) *Trans Bodies, Trans Selves: A Resource for the Transgender Community*. New York: Oxford University Press.

Theron, L. & Collier, K. (2013) "Experiences of female partners of masculine-identifying trans persons." *Culture Health & Sexuality 15*, suppl.

Veldorale-Griffin, A. (2014) "Transgender parents and their adult children's experiences of disclosure and transition." *Journal of GLBT Family Studies 10*, 5, 475–501.

White, T. & Ettner, R. (2007) "Adaptation and adjustment in children of transsexual parents." *European Child and Adolescent Psychiatry 16*, 4, 215–221.

Chapter 5

Fitzgerald, E., Patterson, S.E., Hickey, D., Biko, C., *et al.* (2015) *Meaningful Work: Transgender Experiences in the Sex Trade*. Washington, DC: National Center for Trans Equality.

Whitman-Walker Health (n.d.) *Safer Sex for Trans Bodies*. Accessed on August 6, 2019 at www.whitman-walker.org/Guides%20PDF/Safer%20Sex%20for%20Trans%20Bodies.pdf.

Chapter 6

Cook-Daniels, L. & Munson, M. (2010) "Sexual violence, elder abuse, and sexuality of transgender adults age 50+: Results of three surveys." *Journal of GLBT Family Studies 6*, 2.

Dugan, J. & Fabbre, V. (2018) *To Survive on This Shore*. Heidelberg: Kehrer Verlag.

Filar, R. (2015) *Is It a Man or a Woman? Transitioning and the Cis Gaze.* Accessed on August 6, 2019 at https://rayfilar.wordpress.com/2015/10/15/is-it-a-man-or-a-woman-transitioning-and-the-cis-gaze.

Fredriksen-Goldsen, K.I., Simoni, J.M., Kim, H.J., *et al.* (2014) "The health equity promotion model: reconceptualization of lesbian, gay, bisexual, and transgender (LGBT) health disparities." *American Journal of Orthopsychiatry 84*, 6, 653–663.

Grant, J.M., Mottet, L.A., Tanis, J., Harrison, J., Herman, J.L., & Keisling, M. (2011) *Injustice at Every Turn: A Report of the National Transgender Discrimination Survey.* Washington, DC: National Center for Transgender Equality and National Gay and Lesbian Task Force.

James, S.E., Herman, J.L., Rankin, S., Keisling, M., Mottet, L., & Anafi, M. (2016) *The Report of the 2015 U.S. Transgender Survey.* Washington, DC: National Center for Transgender Equality.

National Center for Transgender Equality (n.d.) *Trans Legal Services Network Directory.* Accessed on August 6, 2019 at https://transequality.org/issues/resources/trans-legal-services-network-directory.

National Center for Transgender Equality (2014) *Know Your Rights: Medicare.* Accessed on July 22, 2019 at https://transequality.org/know-your-rights/medicare.

Persson, D. (2009) "Unique challenges of transgender aging: Implications from the literature." *Journal of Gerontological Social Work 52*, 6, 633–646.

Rodriguez, V.N. (2016) "'I own my T!': The experience of older transgender people of color regarding personal identity, systems of support, and desires for the future." Masters thesis. Accessed on July 22, 2019 at https://scholarworks.smith.edu/theses/1740.

Chapter 8

American Psychological Association (2015) "Guidelines for psychological practice with transgender and gender nonconforming people." *American Psychologist 70*, 9, 832–864.

Congress, E. (2000) "What social workers should know about ethics: Understanding and resolving practice dilemmas." *Advances in Social Work 1*, 1–25.

McAuliffe, D. & Chenoweth, L. (2008) "Leave no stone unturned: The inclusive model of ethical decision making." *Ethics and Social Welfare 2*, 1, 38–49.

Workers, N.A. (2008) *NASW Code of Ethics (Guide to the Everyday Professional Conduct of Social Workers)*. Washington, DC: NASW.

Index